PRAISE FOR DEAN SLUYTER'S

Why the Chicken Crossed the Road
and Other Hidden Enlightenment Teachings
from Buddha to Bebop to Mother Goose

"This is a GREAT book! Sluyter doesn't miss a beat in his praise of the sacred and the profane on the path of spiritual enlightenment."

—*NAPRA Review*

"This smart, sassy, and idiosyncratic spiritual resource is divided into sections on cosmic jokes, sacred nursery rhymes, exploding proverbs, and accidental hymns. . . . Sluyter proves to be a subtle and imaginative guide through the contemporary world of pop culture, dazzling us with epiphanies. . . . He provides fresh takes on faith, devotion, grace, being present, beauty, practice, selflessness, forgiveness, simplicity. Like the best spiritual teachers, Sluyter lets light in from many angles—in this case, the wisdom of Buddhism, Christianity, Taoism and more. *Why the Chicken Crossed the Road* is a surefire demonstration of why play is an essential ingredient in spiritual growth."

—*Values and Visions*

THE ZEN COMMANDMENTS

ALSO BY DEAN SLUYTER

Why the Chicken Crossed the Road
and Other Hidden Enlightenment Teachings
from Buddha to Bebop to Mother Goose

DEAN SLUYTER

ILLUSTRATED BY
MAGGY SLUYTER

JEREMY P. TARCHER/PUTNAM
a member of
PENGUIN PUTNAM INC.
New York

THE ZEN
COMMANDMENTS

Ten Suggestions

for a Life of Inner Freedom

Most Tarcher/Putnam books are available at special quantity discounts for bulk purchase for sales promotions, premiums, fund-raising, and educational needs. Special books or book excerpts also can be created to fit specific needs. For details, write Putnam Special Markets, 375 Hudson Street, New York, NY 10014.

Jeremy P. Tarcher/Putnam
a member of
Penguin Putnam, Inc.
375 Hudson Street
New York, NY 10014
www.penguinputnam.com

Library of Congress Cataloging-in-Publication Data
Sluyter, Dean.
The Zen commandments : ten suggestions for a life of inner freedom
/ Dean Sluyter.
p.   cm.
Includes bibliographical references.
ISBN 1-58542-084-0
1. Spiritual life.   I. Title.
BL624.S55   2001   00-064835
248.4—dc21
Printed in the United States of America

1   3   5   7   9   10   8   6   4   2

This book is printed on acid-free paper. ∞

Book design by Jennifer Ann Daddio

AUTHOR'S NOTE

Not being a Zen master, I've got a lot of nerve writing about Zen. Not being a chosen prophet, I've got chutzpah handing down commandments. But this book is about neither commandments nor Zen per se. It's about the discovery of inner freedom—in Zen, but also in the Gospels, the movies, and a lot of other places—and how this freedom can lead naturally to kindness, without the need to be commanded. So Zen commandments are no commandments, as silent as one hand clapping.

What does that leave? Suggestions: skillful methods for making freedom and kindness vivid in your own life, by your own choice.

—DLS

ACKNOWLEDGMENTS

I am grateful to Charles Genoud, Dan Jackson, Ellen Lewis, Jodi Manning, Sue Murray, Rob Pitera, Mary Rachel Platt, Bob Rusling, Erica Saypol, Maggy Sluyter, Tara Wings Sluyter, and Jim Vincent for their valuable feedback and suggestions. I also wish to thank Gretchen and Bill Richardson for their gracious hospitality, Jane Cavolina for her advice and encouragement, Sean McAnally for the saxophone lessons, the late Coco for keeping me company, and my agent, Jon Matson, for continuing to be a wonderful adviser and friend. Joel Fotinos and Sara Carder of Tarcher/Putnam lent their astute creative support, and my editor, the amazing Jeremy Tarcher, once again pointed the way through the wilderness. Thanks most of all to my family, who keep the party going at all hours and all costs, and to my teachers, whose 84,000 varieties of compassion reveal the translucent perfection of this moment, as is.

FOR MAGGY, DAY, AND TARA

CONTENTS

An' for every hung-up person in the whole wide universe An' we gazed upon the chimes of freedom flashing.

—BOB DYLAN

She hath often dreamed of unhappiness and waked herself with laughing.

—*MUCH ADO ABOUT NOTHING*

THE ZEN COMMANDMENTS

WHAT IT'S
ALL ABOUT

Experiment alone can give certainty.

—ALBERTUS MAGNUS

Some people are waiting for the sun to shine, but not Gene Kelly. As he performs the title song in *Singin' in the Rain*, the weather is imperfect but that's perfectly fine with him. He's not just coping with it, he's celebrating in it—splashing and stomping through puddles the way we did when we were kids, his smiling face turned to the sky, his umbrella (signifying all our sensible, grownup caution) closed and transformed into a graceful dance partner. I think people love this scene because it conveys the uninhibited joy that we somehow feel our lives should be about, even as the storms of messy, uncontrollable circumstances rain down upon us. You'd never guess that Kelly was running a 103-degree fever during filming.

We all probably suspect that such a life is possible. For fleeting moments we may even feel that we've grasped the secret, while reading philosophy or poetry, listening to Bach or Hendrix, scaling the mountain or making love. The light flickers on . . . but then flickers off again.

The big news (which is not new at all) is that we can have that light as a steady brilliance, if we know where to focus. Over the centuries, some people have stumbled onto this discovery, others have carefully stalked it, and their report is outrageous but unanimous. The light—the kingdom of heaven or nirvana or moksha or tawhid or shekina, depending on your preferred vocabulary—is within you. The dimension of boundless freedom and happiness is not in some external sensation or grand achievement, not in some holy person or next world up in the clouds, but within *you*. And it *is* within you— not will be someday or can be if you behave, but *is*, now and always.

And finding this boundless dimension (the report continues) doesn't affect only ourselves. The more we bask in that inner light, the more we radiate it to others. Love, generosity, kindness are its natural overflow. As Gene Kelly sings:

> *I'm laughin' at clouds, so dark up above*
> *The sun's in my heart and I'm ready for love.*

In fact, as he walks off at the end of the song, he passes a fellow pedestrian coming the other way and, barely breaking his stride, hands him the umbrella. It's not enough to sing in the rain ourselves—we've got to pass the torch along to others, perfect strangers included.

INDESCRIBABLY DELICIOUS

Because it's within you, this radiant happiness is nothing exotic, nothing extrasuperduper to be added to life like a deluxe whipped topping, but the nature of life itself, as it is already, which has somehow gone unnoticed. It's there in every moment, haunting your every act, as plain as the nose on your face and just as easily overlooked.

> *He who glows in the depths of your own eyes—that is the Infinite; that is the Self of yourself. He is the Beautiful One, he is the Luminous One. In all the worlds, forever and ever, he shines!*
>
> —CHANDOGYA UPANISHAD

What we call saintly or enlightened people, Christs and Buddhas, have *realized* their inner nature, but everyone has it. All we need is clearer vision—not more concepts or beliefs, but direct experience.

Without that, we're naturally skeptical. We all enjoy the jokes and cartoons in which the cross-legged guru on the mountaintop imparts some bogus secret of life: "You do the Hokey Pokey and you turn yourself around. That's what it's all about." But they wouldn't be funny unless we held a deep conviction that there should be some *real* secret. So we keep projecting symbols of it: Shangri-La, the Holy Grail, the bluebird of happiness, the pot of gold at the end of the rainbow, the major chord at the end of the symphony, the ultimate lover (perhaps in the guise of some movie god or goddess), the ultimate home run or touchdown.

We seem to know it's something indescribable, and indescribably delicious—so delicious that we give it names like "heaven" and "nirvana" and "enlightenment." It's also indescribably simple. I once asked a famous chef the secret of great cooking. He said, "Start with the best ingredients, and then don't screw them up." If the kingdom of nirvana is really within us, we're starting with the very best ingredient of all. We just have to not screw it up, just get it in and out of the sauté pan of daily living without burning it, so that its natural flavor is retained. That involves learning a few simple skills and then practicing them with persistence. My aim in this book is to suggest what those skills might be.

In doing so, I make a point of drawing on any tradition that promotes compassionate outer behavior and enlightened inner awareness. Sometimes I think that on my right wrist I should wear one of those WWJD (What Would Jesus Do?) bracelets, and on my left wrist one that says HWBS (How Would Buddha See?). I'm just interested in *what works*—a sort of dogma-free spiritual street smarts. I'm trying to sum it up in as many points as you can tick off on the fingers of two hands and say, "Here's what it comes down to."

COMMANDMENTS AND SUGGESTIONS

There's a saying that "God gave us Ten Commandments, not Ten Suggestions." OK then, here are Ten Suggestions. Not orders from on high, but practical tips for *getting* high—that is, for raising our awareness and our life to the highest possible state.

I've certainly got nothing against the Commandments. They include some obviously impeccable guidelines for right behavior (as do the Five Precepts, the Six Perfections, and the Eightfold Noble Path, not to mention the Vedic Smritis and the Confucian Analects). But after some 3,000 years of being commanded, people still lie, steal, covet, and all the rest. The Commandments just don't say much about the inner awareness from which outer behavior springs. Do the right thing, of course. But better yet, live so drenched in inner light that doing the right thing comes as naturally as breathing.

> *There is light within a person of light, and it shines on the whole world.*
>
> ——THE GOSPEL OF THOMAS

Live your ethics from the inside out, without requiring that the divine father (or mother) command and threaten you. In short, grow up. Isn't that what all parents want for their children?

In compiling our suggestions, we don't have to start from scratch. We'll illuminate the subject from any number of angles, many of them unknown to our ancestors, from jazz and rock 'n' roll to pointillist painting, from American movies to the inner liberation technologies of Tibet. We'll also loop back, from time to time, to the Ten Commandments, which, when revisited on a deeper level, turn out to offer some surprising enlightenment wisdom of their own.

The main thing is to make our suggestions realistic. We need methods we can actually *use*, vehicles we can ride from where we are. It's all very well to say "Love everyone" or "Be unmoved in loss and gain," but if we could really do that we wouldn't need methods and books. To be useful, the suggestions must pass the Three-in-the-

Morning Test: do they still ring true even in the sleepless hours when people get lonely and scared, when lofty sentiments can seem suddenly hollow? If they sound simplistic, that's all right—sometimes the simplest equations (say $E=mc^2$) have the most spectacular applications.

It's said that Thomas Edison, when he was considering hiring a new assistant, would take him to lunch and watch him closely. If the man salted his food without tasting it first, Edison wouldn't hire him; he'd know he wasn't a good scientist. I invite you to be a good scientist. Don't accept or reject anything out of hand, but check it out, test it in the laboratory of your own experience—taste it as it actually is before salting it with preconceptions.

> You shall no longer take things at second or third hand,
>   nor look through the eyes of the dead, nor feed on
>   the specters in books,
> You shall not look through my eyes either, nor take
>   things from me,
> You shall listen to all sides and filter them from your-
> self.
>
> —WALT WHITMAN

And if, after due experimentation, you find that the formulas I've set forth here don't work for you, by all means look elsewhere. These are, after all, just suggestions—they're not written in stone.

But if you do connect with them, I invite you to apply them wholeheartedly. We're talking about a complete transformation of our lives, and that won't come from a superficial commitment. Be warned: enlightenment is the most seductive of lovers. What begins as a casual flirtation eventually takes everything you've got.

In other words, you put your whole self in and you shake it all about. The cartoon guru is right after all. When you do *this* Hokey Pokey, you really *do* turn yourself around: you reorient your life by 180 degrees, so that, no matter what's raining on you, you're always luxuriating in that brilliant inner sun and shining it forth for others.

And that's what it's all about.

1.

REST IN
OPENNESS

No beer left.

I'll sit and drink

The sky.

—JOSH FEUER

I grew up about a mile from the spot where the pivotal scene of *Gone with the Wind* was filmed—the one where Scarlett O'Hara, starving and desperate, shakes her fist at the sky and swears, "As God is my witness, I'll never be hungry again!" Through the rest of the film we watch her fulfill her vow . . . sort of. She struggles to attain the perfect home, business, marriage, and family, she gets everything she sets her sights on, yet none of it works out quite the way she had hoped. There's always some problem, and her hunger is never satisfied. As the movie ends, she's still scheming: "After all, tomorrow is another day."

Sometimes it seems as if, like Scarlett, we're spending our lives dealing with problems and hustling for the things that are supposed to fulfill us. Yet fulfillment is always just beyond our grasp, in some indefinite tomorrow. The First Suggestion addresses this predicament.

A PARABLE

Consider the waves of the ocean.

At any given moment, a wave is limited in space: extending from Point A to Point B, it's just so big and no bigger, isolated by the troughs that separate it from other waves. It's also limited in time: it arose at some moment in the past and will crash against the shore at some moment in the future. And it's never at rest but is in constant, turbulent motion.

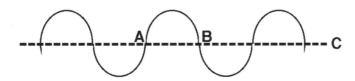

Like waves, all the things I encounter are limited, isolated, and in motion, and so am I. From *my* Point A to Point B is just 5'10" and 153 pounds, and not only my body but my personality, history, philosophy, social status, net worth—everything I might identify with Me is dwarfed by the much larger totality of Not Me. Within the great expanse of time it's a frighteningly short span from the moment of my birth to the moment when I will crash against the shore we call death. And both I and all the other finite, wavelike beings undergo the turbulence of constant activity and change, often creating new problems and limitations as we slosh up against each other.

Most of us respond to this situation by looking for ways to swell up our Me wave as big as possible. If I can inflate myself with just a few more buckets of money, knowledge, affection, muscles, prestige, sharper clothes, cooler attitudes, more intense sensations, maybe I'll finally overcome limitation and become the King of All Waves. Or maybe I can overcome the ravages of time and death by freezing all waves in place—after I get them to stop sloshing and line up *my* way. Then everything will stay the way I want it and I'll live forever.

But history books and the tragedies of Shakespeare are full of people trying these strategies, and they haven't worked yet. Perhaps, then, I might be ready to try a new strategy. I can begin by noticing that I've considered only the surface of life, the world above Dotted Line C. If I look beneath it, I find that something underlies my little wave—the vast ocean, from which I arise and into which I eventually subside.

You cannot conceive the many without the one.

—PLATO

Unlike waves, the ocean is not limited to puny sizes and shapes, and while wave after wave crashes into oblivion, the ocean lives on. What's more, the ocean connects every wave to every other wave, dissolving isolation, and it's immune to the turbulence of change—even when there are tempests at the surface, the ocean rests in its bed in perfect tranquility.

What I want to do, then, is be more like the ocean. What separates me from it? Amazingly, nothing. The closer we look for the division between wave and ocean, the clearer it becomes that there isn't any. Dotted Line C is merely an imaginary structure in a diagram. In fact, there's no such "thing" as a wave, no such limited, self-existent object. It's just a function of the limitless ocean, a way the ocean expresses itself. So my quest to overcome limitation has been misdirected all along. Instead of trying to swell my wave higher or manipulate the other waves to suit me, I can just settle into my overlooked base till I fully experience that I've been ocean all along.

Of course this is just an analogy (and a very old one, by the way). What *is* that ocean? Here words tend to break down. We can say it's not anything that is, but the is-ness by which all things are. We can say it's the boundless awareness-space within which all boundaries are experienced. We can also say it's what you really want whenever you think you want anything else. Or we can say it's where the sound of the bell goes as it fades into silence, where the knot goes when it's untied, where the steeple goes as it tapers into the sky. And if we like this kind of language, we can say it's the kingdom of God, the ground of Being, the Over-soul, Brahman (vastness), shunyata (emptiness), Tao, Allah, infinity, eternity.

> *"I don't call it anything,"*
> *Said Frankie Lee with a smile.*
> —BOB DYLAN

Since all names are inadequate anyway, perhaps that's our wisest course—to agree not to label it and focus instead on how to experience it. We're not talking about believing in the ocean or singing its praises, but being good scientists and checking out the situation for ourselves through direct, immediate experience—diving *into* the ocean.

LAB "WORK"

How can we dive in? Essentially, by letting go and doing nothing. Anything else will result in our splashing around and churning water, creating more turbulence. Instead, we need to take a break from all that doing and just rest. Of course, we already rest when we sleep, but then we fall unconscious and stop experiencing. Instead, we need to *consciously* do nothing, take it easy alertly, repose in wide-awakeness: REST IN OPENNESS.

So, time for some lab work . . . or, rather, nonwork. Please sit someplace where you're comfortable and out of people's way.

OK?

Pull your shoulders up to your ears and then drop them. Settle into the seat—let it take all your weight. Because we're so used to speeding along on the expressway of doing, we can start with a bit of breathing practice as a sort of deceleration lane, an offramp to nondoing. Take a slow, full breath, hold it for a few moments, then let out a deep sigh, as if breathing out through all your pores, letting go of everything, all burdens and decisions, stress and distress: *Ahhh!* Do this a few times.

Then just sit. That's all. Don't try to concentrate on anything or feel a certain way. Don't resist thoughts or pursue them; as they arise, just let them go. Simply continue to *be*—just relax and remain aware, naturally open, as you already are. Practice this way for a little while, and then we'll discuss it further.

Nothing to it . . . literally.

In Zen this alert nondoing is called *shikantaza,* "just sitting." People often call it "meditation," but again we're probably better off not calling it anything. Otherwise, it can sound like something that requires effort: concentrating on this, blocking out that, assuming solemn attitudes or adopting arcane beliefs—all merely new, improved ways to churn the water. Instead we just sit, just be, and let whatever happens happen.*

NO CIGAR

In fact, openness exists naturally, from moment to moment of our actual lives, while sitting practice just attunes us to *recognize* it in those moments. You could be walking down a forest path or a supermarket aisle, singing in the choir or slamming in the mosh pit, tooling down Pacific Coast Highway on your Harley or crawling through the Lincoln Tunnel in your Chevy—as long as your awareness is open wide and you're resting in each moment of simple experience, allowing it to unfold spontaneously.

---

*For more on sitting, please see Appendix, page 177.

I am become a transparent eyeball; I am nothing; I see all; the currents of the Universal Being circulate through me. . . .

—EMERSON

We're all attracted to activities we find conducive to this union of alertness and restfulness. For some people golf or gardening, dancing or shooting hoops, taking Communion or sitting back with a cigar provides just the right balance of elements. My father was always happiest when he was sailing his boat in the Catalina Channel, vigilantly trimming his sails while serenely losing himself in the clear horizon. We can't sail our boats all the time, but by resting in openness we can sail through life. We can develop a new habit of attentive tranquility that is content-free—like sitting back with a cigar, only without the cigar.

So the way to boundless experience is to not seek boundless experience or *any* particular experience beyond whatever presents itself. This nonseeking does take practice, not to get "better" at "doing" it, since there's no doing involved, but to give our old seeking habit some road upon which to run out of gas. Sooner or later, we give up and just let the infinite (or whatever you want to call it) engulf us. By definition, the infinite is everywhere and everything; ocean can never be absent from even the smallest drop of wave. We've simply been distracted from it by our constant compulsion to look somewhere else for something more.

PUSHING, PULLING, AND FREEDOM

This one change changes everything. As we gradually learn to leave off distractedness and rest in openness, we stop looking for fulfillment outside of the way things already are. Till now we've gone through life *pushing* and *pulling*—trying to push the undesirable away from us and pull the desirable toward us. It's such an entrenched habit that we persist even when there's no payoff, when it only creates frustration. Stuck in the traffic jam, we keep trying to push the cars out of the way with our mental bulldozer; spotting the luscious babe (or hunk), we keep trying to extend our mental tendrils and pull her (or him) within copulation range.

But resting in openness, free from the agitation of pushing and pulling, we can just witness the situation. This doesn't mean to suppress our anger at the traffic if it arises or our lust for the babe if it arises, for those arisings are also part of the situation we're witnessing. But it means we don't get lost in the arisings either, don't fixate on them.

Elevate the scope of 360-degree global awareness.

—LAMA SURYA DAS

To be open is to be receptive to all 360 degrees of our experience, not stuck in the five or ten degrees where we're pushing or pulling.

Watch a child get a vaccination and see how he ignores the hundreds of square inches of skin surface that feel fine, perversely squeezing his whole attention into the hundredth of a square inch that's in pain. Most of us are experts at this, fixating on our stresses and traumas, maintaining them as carefully as an album of family photos.

> *We tend our pain meticulously through the familiar process of thinking about it. The more we think around our emotional pain the more we cripple ourselves with the artificial intensity of it. . . . We could allow our pain to dissolve into the skylike openness of direct experience; but somehow we feel more secure with our pain as a reference point.*
>
> —NGAK'CHANG RINPOCHE

Now, though, as we grow increasingly at home with that 360-degree "skylike openness of direct experience," we find our cozy habit of cultivating and magnifying problems melting into it like summer clouds.

Being open to 360 degrees doesn't mean keeping track of everything, like some kind of fish-eye security camera. Whenever we notice we're fixating we just let go, and then remain naturally receptive to whatever appears. We can also reclaim this receptivity a few degrees at a time. For example, right now, take a few moments and notice all the layers of sound (the voices in the next room, the air conditioner or the radiator or the rain dripping off the leaves . . .). Or notice the full range of your peripheral vision, which is surprisingly wide; then, each time you realize that your visual attention has narrowed into its old tunnel, relax out into its full range again. Or as you sit through a lecture or a business meeting, notice your tactile sense: the pressure of your butt against the chair and your feet against the floor, the varied textures of clothing against your skin, the temperature of the air on your face and hands. Or notice thoughts and feelings as they emerge, shift, and vanish—notice how they, in a way, are also sense objects of a subtler kind.

THE END OF BOREDOM

As panoramic receptivity gradually replaces limited fixation, every situation becomes a glimpse of limitlessness. Let's say you're stuck at a red light and you find yourself gripping the wheel, straining subtly forward, fixated on trying to make the red light turn green. Of course straining can't turn the light green a moment sooner, although it may turn your knuckles white. So rest in openness instead. Liberated from pushing and pulling, from trying to turn the situation into what it isn't, sit back and relax into the richness of what is—the weight of your body against the seat, the morning light glinting off glass and chrome, the chug of idling engines, and the multicolored river of car bodies, each enfolding the mysterious, shadowy figure of a driver.

And maybe, with your freer vision, you'll even notice that you can cut over a block to a clearer street. By helping us see out of our ruts, openness leads to open-mindedness, receptivity to new experiences and ideas. It does this by freeing us from a third habit, along with pushing and pulling: *ignoring*, the screening out of "irrelevant" experiences that aren't obviously desirable or undesirable. Then the mind starts to function in a more playful, fluid, creative way, to explore the wide world of possibilities beyond the horizon of our old thoughts and plans, to notice overlooked solutions and wonderful surprises.

The end men looked for cometh not,
And a path there is where no man thought.

—EURIPIDES, *MEDEA*

As we unlearn the habit of ignoring, we regain the freshness of a child's perception. (Jesus said, "Unless you change and become like children, you will never enter the kingdom of heaven.") We again behold in wonder the dust particles that swim in a sunbeam, or an airplane as it miraculously hums and booms across the sky, or our own surrealistically foreshortened reflection in the toaster or cereal spoon. We again see magical shapes in the clouds, even as we seamlessly handle our grownup responsibilities. There's no conflict between these two modes: we can be childlike without being childish.

If, when hearing that I have been stilled at last,
    they stand at the door,
Watching the full-starred heavens that winter sees,
Will this thought rise on those who will meet my face no
    more,
"He was one who had an eye for such mysteries"?

—THOMAS HARDY

Life, it turns out, is never stale. What made it *seem* stale was our pushing, pulling, and ignoring it. "Boredom," says Ram Dass, "is just lack of attention." In this perpetual freshness of open attention, you don't need to keep jumping off bridges on a bungee cord or jumping into bed with different partners just to know you're alive. Compulsions and addictions naturally start falling away. You can, if you like, be a Buddha of the Burbs, mowing the lawn in summer amazement, shoveling the snow in winter amazement. Your life regains and retains that new-car smell.

UNBUSYING

All this comes from just resting open to each moment as it is. Ironically, though, such ease requires vigilance—our penchant for getting caught up in things is so powerful. One of my teachers recommends deliberately interrupting our busy-ness at least fifty or sixty times a day.

> *When you find yourself in the thick of it*
> *Help yourself to a bit of what is all around you.*
> —LENNON/McCARTNEY

If you have an alarm on your watch, you can set it to go off at odd intervals and remind you to take an awareness break, even for a few seconds. When you're watching television or working at a computer, occasionally look away from the screen, breathe out *(Ahhh!)*, let your mind decompress, and simply be, relaxing into the panorama of the moment's experience. When you're caught up in an intense, engrossing conversation, air it out with tiny, sporadic moments of silence in which you let the forgotten, wider totality of existence break through. When your awareness feels pinched by the pressure of some problematic life situation, step back from the problem, drop out of the pinchedness, hang out in openness.

Does this opening up and dropping out sound like spacing out—evading responsibility? Actually, by refreshing the mind, it helps us deal with life more effectively. Our responsibilities are still there; we just start to see them in a wider perspective. True, we may see that many things we worried about are out of our hands. Then we can conscientiously handle the things we can do something about and let the rest go, rather than keep bashing our heads against them. But that's a good thing—that's a relief.

Fortunately, we're not in control.

—WILLIE NELSON

OUT OF EGYPT

In fact, this dropping-out process is so important, it's mandated in the Ten Commandments:

Remember the sabbath day, and keep it holy.

The sabbath is the day of rest, and to keep something holy is to use it as a means of opening to the infinite. The whole idea of sabbath is a temporary withdrawal from limited worldly activities (waves) in order to reconnect with the limitlessness (ocean) that some people call God. Here we're practicing this principle on the most profound level, resting not only one day out of seven and not only from the physical activities of our jobs, but gradually learning to be in a state of utter rest seven days a week, sixty seconds a minute, transcending and silently witnessing all physical and mental activities, even while performing them.

Then we also fulfill the First Commandment:

I am the Lord your God, who brought you out of
the land of Egypt, out of the house of slavery. You shall
have no other gods before Me.

The Hebrew word for Egypt, *Mitzraim,* is a plural noun with associated meanings of "confines, constrictions, narrow places," as well as "anguish, distress, worries." Thus the first sentence can be read: "I am the ultimate reality, the wide-open limitlessness that has freed you from the anguish of all narrow limitations." Note that the phrase "brought you out," past tense, implies that we're already free. There's nothing for us to *do,* just refrain from *re*-enslaving ourselves, from getting caught up again in pushing and pulling at the multitude of limited experiences; stop submitting to their power, making them "other gods" as if *they* were ultimate. Instead let go (as Moses tells Pharaoh), rest in openness, and experience that the only ultimate is the one that is right here, now, amidst all the limitations. We could paraphrase the Commandment as: "I am the supreme, oceanic boundlessness that has saved you from all wavelike turbulence and constriction. Don't go back to it by mistaking any single wave for the whole ocean."

TAKING OUT THE TRASH

Well then. What does it all come down to?
Taking out the trash.
After all this fancy cosmic talk, there you are, taking out the

trash again—perhaps not one of your favorite activities. This presents you with a choice. You can grumble, narrowing your awareness into a vaccination-sized throb of resentment. Or you can distract yourself with a fantasy of being elsewhere (like those bumper stickers: I'D RATHER BE WATERSKIING). Or, instead, you can rest from both resentment and fantasy, and open into the awareness of what's actually there—the weight of the trash bag pulling on the muscles of your arm, footstep on gravel, footstep on gravel, footstep on gravel, the smell of night air, the receding of the noise and business within the house, the crickets or cicadas or rumbling traffic, the stars or fog or moonlit clouds, and perhaps a taste of the subtle, silent, indefinable Whatsis behind it all. Suddenly it's as rich an experience as you could possibly want.

The mundane is the sublime. Jesus says, "Knock and it shall be opened unto you." That is, give your undistracted attention to whatever presents itself, and its stubborn opaqueness will open unto you, revealing glorious transparency. One Zen practitioner described this experience as feeling "free as a fish in an ocean of cool, clear water after being stuck in a tank of glue."

To see it, there's never anything else you need or need to get rid of, not a pinch more or less than whatever's at hand. Wherever you are is the perfect place to rest in openness. Everything's grist for the mill, as long as the mill wheel is turning—as long as you're paying effortless, panoramic attention. Then it's all vast openness: washing the dishes, cleaning the kitty litter, listening to annoying political opinions, making love or stubbing your toe, dying or being born. You'll forget a million times, and a million and one times you'll remember: Oh, yes . . . this is it . . . just this . . . rest in this.

Everything points to it. It fills all directions. We peer through telescopes to see into the depths of space, but we're *in* deep space all along—there's nowhere else to be. Contemplating a mountain plateau or a sparkling sea may give us some feel for openness, but the real thing is everywhere, even in the most cluttered storeroom or crowded subway car. It has (it *is*) unlimited room for everything, including all our clutter and claustrophobia, without ever becoming a drop less vast.

> *Enlightenment is nothing other than the spontaneous experience of all possible structures as equivalent to open space.*
>
> —PRAJNAPARAMITA SUTRA

When everything is equivalent to open space, nothing impinges on us. We finally discover that all the closedness that we thought was hemming us in was a mistake of perception—a sort of optical illusion. Every little wave is measureless ocean, including the one called Me.

> *You, therefore, are the infinite. "I am not the infinite" is a mere illusion. From illusion springs separation wherein all sorrows have root.*
>
> —SHANKARACHARYA

So . . . what? So enjoy being, and cut the root of sorrows. Sit down and "meditate" in silence; get up and navigate through activity; either way, just relax and remain aware. That's it—your job is done. Again and again, and with growing clarity, we discover that, *no matter what's going on,* we can find perfect freedom by resting in openness to the totality of present awareness. As long as we're caught up in this or that, pushing or pulling, trick or treat, we're in the land of Mitzraim, the house of slavery. As long as we're resting in openness, wherever we are is the Promised Land.

> *The narrow straits of our tribulation are limited: but*
> *the large way whereby we pass along hath no end.*
>
> —SAINT AUGUSTINE

2.

ACT WITH
KINDNESS

*Life's persistent and most urgent question is, "What
are you doing for others?"*

—REV. MARTIN LUTHER KING, JR.

Squirrels are pretty smart, but not as smart as I once thought. I used
to be amazed at their ability to bury acorns in my lawn in the fall,
remember where they had stashed them, and then return in winter
to dig them up. Then one day my wife read that they *don't* remember:
they just dig at random until they get lucky.

People are something like squirrels in winter, digging not only
for the means of survival but for things like security, meaning, love.
Somehow these buried treasures seem mislaid, out of sight, and the
digging is pretty much hit-or-miss. What we've learned from the
First Suggestion (unbelievably, impossibly) is that the whole lawn is
one big acorn—if we can open wide enough to swallow and digest
it. But what about all those other hungry squirrels? Having found

the tranquil kingdom of heaven within, must we come back out to the world of problems?

The fact is, we're already there. As long as we have a body, as long as we're sucking up oxygen and food, we're in the lifestream, like it or not, interacting with the world and all the beings in it. Every carrot or veal chop we eat sends ripples of implication throughout the planet; even if we live in a cave, our every breath exchanges molecules with species we've never heard of. So our decision is not *whether* to interact, but *how.* The answer is simple in principle, but often difficult and complex in practice. As E.T. tells little Drew Barrymore in his parting instruction: "Be good."

Usually our prime concern is ourselves. Maybe it's because of the way self-preservation is neurologically hardwired into our systems, but when there's just one slice of hot lasagna left in the cafeteria, my first impulse is to grab it quick, before the next guy does. Some serious ethical conditioning might override that desire and cause me to leave it for him. But could there be a way for unselfishness itself to be my desire, for kindness to rise from the depths of my being as authentically and as powerfully as hunger?

One useful starting point is the question, Who would you die for?

> *No one has greater love than this,*
> *to lay down one's life for one's friends.*
> —JOHN 15:13

To give up your life is to give up *all* future lasagna, all symphonies and sunsets, all the body parts you've fought the germs to preserve, all the wisdom you've struggled to attain—yet soldiers do die for their countries and most parents would die for their children. If we can imagine even one scenario in which we would sacrifice our life for others, it means we're potentially capable of the ultimate altruism. And that means we're capable of all the more modest, everyday forms of altruism that constitute being good.

TAKING THE PLUNGE

But how can we mobilize that potential? Mainly, we just do it. Every day is filled with opportunities to be generous—materially, emotionally, with our talents, with our time. There's no need to wait around for some revelation or transformation; just take the plunge. You can work up to the big, difficult things by starting with things that are small and difficult: letting the car slip in ahead of you from the side street, giving up your seat on the bus, passing up that lasagna. Every time you do, there's a sensation of shattering boundaries, of breaking into the clear, wide-open space that lies outside the small space of self-interest.

There are also mind techniques that can help shatter those boundaries. One is an intensified variation on the old idea of walking a mile in someone else's shoes, called "exchanging self for others."

If I were you, you would love me.
—GRAFFITO SPOTTED IN THE HAGUE

Sit down, close your eyes, and imaginatively inhabit another person's name, situation, and skin. Take plenty of time to settle into it, letting that be your "self" and seeing how it feels. And while you're there, notice how you're still driven by exactly the same desire to be happy and avoid suffering that drives you now. Repeated practice of this technique makes it increasingly difficult to regard others as alien forces—it reinforces the experience that we're expressions of the *same* force, the same desire. (You can also do this technique with nonhuman beings. The expression "He wouldn't hurt a fly" starts to become meaningful when you've tried *being* a fly.)

Another method is again to close the eyes and this time visualize a balance scale, with yourself sitting at one end and all the other beings in the universe at the other. Watch which end of the scale drops and which rises, and then ask, Who is more important?

You can also sit down and think about all the people who have shown you kindness in your life—the schoolteacher who took the time to encourage you, the friend who was there to talk you through a crisis or trauma—and imagine what your life would have been like without all those kind acts. Then ask, How can I not do likewise?

This shift in perspective is further facilitated by simply resting in openness. As we start to find happiness in simply being, we feel less compelled to grab the lasagna in a quest for fulfillment—we're already fulfilled. As our cup gradually runneth over, we find ourselves less preoccupied with filling it, and our cup becomes a fountain for others. This is why we're right to equate enlightened awareness with compassionate behavior. One of my teachers tells a story about the time when, as a young seeker in Nepal, he started having intensely blissful meditative experiences and thought they must indicate some kind of momentous spiritual progress. He sat down with his teacher, a seasoned old Tibetan lama, and began to describe the experiences. The lama cut him off with a single question: "Have they increased your compassion for all beings?" Well, no, they hadn't. "Then they don't mean a thing."

DON'T BE CRUEL

Compassion is not mere pity. From roots that literally mean "suffering with," it's the gut knowledge that the distress of others is real.

> *I feel your pain.*
> —BILL CLINTON

Of course we don't literally, physically feel the other person's pain, but we can come to know that it's *as* real, that it matters as much *as if* we felt it. That realization, the core of the ethical sense, doesn't fully develop (say some psychologists) until about the age of six or seven. But in a sense we still don't get it, *can't* get it as long as our awareness is identified with this narrow piece of real estate we call "me." We can sit right next to a friend who has a throbbing toothache: for him the whole world feels, looks, tastes, smells like toothache, while for us, just on the other side of his skin, the pain is almost absurdly unreal. Compassion means recognizing that there's awareness like ours on his side of the skin.

As we come to experience that you and I are not two wave-objects but one awareness-ocean, we grow less capable of harming one another, more naturally inclined to help one another. This is why the word "selfless" can mean either altruistic or enlightened: eventually they're the same thing. The deepest kind of altruism involves no heroic sacrifice—it's as natural as the right hand pulling the left hand out of the fire. Elvis sang, "Don't be cruel to a heart that's true." The truest hearts are those that have realized the truth of their own nonseparate identity. They *can't* be cruel; they *must* be kind.

But that's a pretty rarefied ideal. The gulf between "them" and "me" will probably feel real for quite some time. The beggar doesn't care how authentically compassionate my dollar is; he's cold, and he wants that bowl of soup (or that bottle of wine) tonight. And by acting *as if* I were compassionate, I may even be able to start feeling my way into the groove of true compassion.

> *Assume a virtue, if you have it not. . . .*
> *For use almost can change the stamp of nature.*
>
> —*HAMLET*

In fact, the most authentic kind of compassion is rare enough that there are special names for those who live it: righteous ones, buddhas, bodhisattvas, saints. But saints aren't special people sent from the heavens—that lets the rest of us off the hook too easily. They're ordinary people who point themselves in the direction of goodness and keep putting one foot in front of the other till it takes them all the way. If you've made the commitment to keep going, it almost doesn't matter how far you've gotten: the outcome is assured. In Buddhism, this compassionate resolve is expressed in the Vow of the Bodhisattva:

> *As long as space remains,*
> *As long as sentient beings remain,*
> *May I too remain*
> *And dispel the miseries of the world.*

This is the longest of long-term commitments—stretching over innumerable life situations and (if there is such a thing) over innumerable lifetimes—to abide in the world of problems until, with our help, all others have found the place where all problems dissolve. That might sound like a cosmic abstraction, but there's always an immediate, concrete application.

> *As long as the space of this marriage, this family, this*
> *job, this project, this friendship, this community*
> *remains,*
> *As long as the others are still dealing with problems,*
> *May I remain on the case*
> *And be part of the solution.*

The truth is, we're all interdependent anyway, materially as well as spiritually. We have always depended upon the kindness of strangers, but especially now, in this age of global economies and precarious ecologies, we can't secure anyone's well-being unless we secure everyone's. And we can't uncover our true identity unless we uncover everyone's, because it's the same identity, the same ocean. The sage Shantideva said:

> *One should always look straight at sentient beings as if*
> *drinking them in with the eyes, thinking, "Relying on*
> *them alone, I shall attain buddhahood."*

This is not just a poetic fancy, but another technique, to be practiced quite literally and rigorously. Among other things, it means that whether or not you give money to the beggar, you don't avert your eyes.

REDUNDANT AND REDUNDANT

The Dalai Lama says that to fulfill the bodhisattva vow could take billions of aeons, but that's OK because you would be spending your time in the most positive way possible; whereas if you're just wasting your time, even one day is too long. The definitive film on this point is *Groundhog Day*, in which Bill Murray plays a mean-spirited, self-centered TV weatherman. ("I'll give you a winter prediction: it's gonna be cold, it's gonna be gray, and it's gonna last you for the rest of your life.") On a visit to Punxsutawney, Pennsylvania, home of Punxsutawney Phil, the famous weather-forecasting groundhog, he finds himself trapped in a time warp, living the same February 2 over and over again. This prison of pointless, endless redundancy is a fitting metaphor for the way people often feel about their lives.

> *Tomorrow and tomorrow and tomorrow*
> *Creeps in this petty pace from day to day*
> *To the last syllable of recorded time. . . .*
>
> — *MACBETH*

In his efforts to escape, our hero tries every kind of selfishness and exploitation. Finally, after exhausting all other possibilities, he tries being kind—beginning with the homeless man he has walked past in all the previous editions of his day. This lifts the spell. Kindness, it turns out, is the way to liberate not only others but ourselves. Significantly, the hero is named Phil, like the groundhog: what immobilizes us is our own shadow, our own projected darkness, and that's what perpetuates the cold grayness of our lives. (The movie takes us through exactly forty-two Groundhog Days, extending the winter of Phil's discontent by the traditional six weeks.) As we begin to project light instead, we light our own path and move along.

In 19th-century Brazil, slaves who escaped from the plantations formed their own small enclaves in the countryside. There they developed the fighting art of Capoeira, disguised as a form of dance. Then, it is said, some of them deliberately allowed themselves to be recaptured so that they could secretly teach it to other slaves, toward the day when they could rise up in a universal revolt. Whether you call it being a saint or a bodhisattva, a hero or a *chutzpanik*, that's the real deal.

> *Kindness is my religion.*
> —H. H. THE XIV DALAI LAMA

ESSAY QUESTIONS

Acting with kindness puts us in compliance with the universal *thou shalt not*'s of all cultures, rejecting murder, rape, theft, all those gross, obvious, willful wrongs—real, deliberate wickedness. But there are also many ethical gray areas where it's difficult to calculate whether we're doing right on some ultimate balance sheet. We're against killing and violence—fine. Then should we all be vegetarians? Then is capital punishment ever OK? Or war? Or abortion? Can you be "pro-life" if you smoke cigarettes? Or if your pension fund is heavily invested in tobacco stocks? Is it moral to pay for designer vitamins while millions of people go hungry? What about trying to protect your family by driving them around in a heavy SUV that endangers everyone else on the road? These are the essay questions—there's no simple true or false. (In the Talmudic tradition, some ethical problems, even after centuries of debate, are given a good Jewish shrug and tagged *TEIKU*, an acronym for, "It will be resolved when Elijah returns.")

So we must take responsibility for our actions; *we* must decide what constitutes kindness. It's just not good enough to say that the Bible (or the Koran or the Sutras or the Vedas) tells us to do this or that. The Bible has been cited to support slavery, to oppose anesthesia for women in childbirth, to condemn other people's ways of making love. *Everyone* who reads scripture reads interpretively and selectively. We're shocked to hear about adulterers being executed in Afghanistan, but that's straight out of the Old Testament, along with the guidelines for selling your daughters into bondage and the mandatory death penalty for cursing your parents or working on Saturday. We're always choosing our own path; the honest thing is to acknowledge it. (An Episcopal bishop in California used to jokingly offer, for a dollar, to find a biblical text to support any position on any issue.)

Of course it would be nice if it were all cut and dried—if, say, the Ten Commandments were the be-all and end-all of ethical behavior. But Judaism has hundreds of divinely ordained laws: one page after the Commandments we're being told under what circumstances an ox should be stoned to death. Christianity gave no special importance to the Commandments until the 13th century; Jesus reportedly endorsed only five, plus one that's not among the Ten (see

Matthew 19:18–19, Mark 10:19). The original texts don't even contain the phrase "Ten Commandments" or number them, and Judaism and various Christian denominations disagree about how to do so. So even that nice, round number ten, with its air of absolute moral authority, is a bit of an invention.

We want our guru to tell us whether to eat hamburgers, or our priest to tell us about family planning, or our rabbi to tell us whether to give to the beggar. We like that cozy feeling of certainty. But coziness can lull us to sleep—uncertainty wakes us up. Each uneasy confrontation with the beggar helps shake us and wake us. And if we're awake and honest with ourselves, we can always know if we're acting from kindness of heart or from its opposite. If you have younger siblings, for example, as a child you might have found many creative ways to make them cry, just for the fun of it. That means you know what deliberate cruelty feels like, and you know when you're consciously making choices that hurt others, from petty social snubs to large-scale environmental crimes.

THE VOICE AND THE DANCE

Socrates said he had an inner voice that guided him, telling him when an action he was considering was wrong. I think we all have that voice, that intuitive sense when we're choosing to be obstinate or self-righteous or cruel. Socrates just *listened*. But we ignore that voice at our peril; every time we do we wind up paying— guaranteed—and not necessarily because some cosmic scorekeeper is meting out punishments, but because the universe is a closed system. Since we're all connected in this ocean, in one form or another everything we do comes back to us.

No man can put a chain about the ankle of his fellow man without at last finding the other end fastened about his own neck.

—FREDERICK DOUGLASS

One method of tuning to that inner voice is through a person who embodies it for you—a role model. It's like dancing with a really good partner. By a sort of osmosis, you get the overall rhythm and feel of the dance more easily than by looking down at your feet and mechanically piecing out the step. The role model could be anyone who makes you say, "Yep, that's what it looks like, that's how it's done." Then you can try to emulate, say, the uninhibited warmth she showers on everyone she meets, her refusal to bear grudges, the easygoing way she says, "I don't know." When you're provoked by rude drivers and find yourself about to respond rudely, you can imagine her sitting beside you in the passenger seat—not scolding, but gently laughing over the way you have once again let yourself get caught by something so small.

And still, sometimes the road rage wins. The truth is, it's a long-term project: over and over again, we just have to keep choosing kindness. At the end of each day you can take a few minutes to do what Saint Ignatius Loyola called the *examen*, mentally reviewing your day, noting where your actions were worthy and where they fell short, and considering how you can do better the next day. There's always a range of actions of which we're capable. Above a certain threshold we can't be that saintly (yet), and below another threshold we can't be that vicious (anymore). The trick is to keep *leaning*, gently but steadily, toward the uppermost level of your range. That way you're always doing the best that can be done by the person you are today and pushing your upper threshold a little higher for tomorrow.

GOOD INTENTIONS

Once, when I was very small, I saw Felix the Cat on TV put a tack on an old man's chair. The victim sat down, then suddenly grabbed his bottom and proceeded to bounce, in lovely, high-arcing parabolas, till he vanished over the horizon. "Neat!," I thought. "I want to see Daddy do that!" Daddy didn't bounce even once. I suppose the spanking I received was a necessary lesson in the difference between the physics of the cartoon world and those of the human world, as well as a deterrent against further television-inspired violence; but still I know my heart was pure. (Buddhist doctrine agrees, holding that we don't incur the full load of negative karma unless we intend to do wrong, we commit the wrongful act, and we take satisfaction in it.)

Still, good intentions pave the road to hell. Kindness must be guided by alert intelligence; it must include *consideration*, the habit of considering the actual consequences of what we do. Otherwise, noble, vague sentiments can result in clumsy blundering. Not long ago in England, some well-intentioned animal-rights activists "liberated" hundreds of domestic minks from a ranch. Unfortunately, the minks had no idea how to survive in the wild. Many wound up starving, dying in accidents, or fatally attacking other animals.

Our crusade was so stupid, only an idealist could have thought of it.

—INGMAR BERGMAN, *THE SEVENTH SEAL*

Our time and resources in this life are limited. It's up to us to use them intelligently, in a way that enhances others' happiness, or at least doesn't add to their suffering. If we could just refrain from *un-kindness*, that would be a lot. We are the agency through which the kingdom comes on earth as it is in heaven. We are the ones who must transform the world, starting with ourselves. We can argue about whether there's some kind of divine Santa Claus waiting in the wings, but there's certainly plenty of need for us all to be Santa's little helpers. It would be very nice to love everyone, and perhaps someday we will. But the great heroism that we can practice right now is to be kind even to those we do not love.

Somebody once asked Aldous Huxley what he had learned from all his years of studying deeply in philosophy and religion. He answered, "Try to be a bit nicer to people." The first time I read this I laughed at its inanity. But of course this is the heart of the matter. Your mission, should you decide to accept it, is to take up every opportunity to give away that possession you want to keep, do that task you don't want to do, help those people you can't abide. And as Jewish wisdom teaches, rather than expect their gratitude you should be grateful to them for giving you the opportunity to do a *mitzvah*, a kindness.

It's not easy, but that's the point: when it's hard it busts your boundaries, it opens you up. And you don't have to do it all at once. You can start by chipping around the edges.

OK

The First and Second Suggestions are the essence of all the others, the two-step dance of liberated life. If (unlike me) you've perfected them, you can skip the rest of this book (and all other books). Phrased a little differently, these two steps are found in all the great spiritual traditions. In the Bible, they are the two Great Laws:

> *You shall love the Lord your God with all your heart,*
> *and with all your soul, and with all your mind. . . .*
> *You shall love your neighbor as yourself.*

That is, open yourself completely to the oceanic infinite, which is always right here; and give yourself completely to the other wavelike beings, who are made of the same oceanwater as you. In Judaism, these two principles are symbolized by the skyward-pointing and earthward-pointing triangles of the Star of David. In the Sutras, where they are called Great Wisdom and Great Compassion, they are symbolized by the image of the Buddha, whose left hand holds a begging bowl (passively open to the vast sky of being) while his right hand touches the ground (actively engaged in the world of doing).

By a happy coincidence, this essence teaching is also summed up in the all-American mantra, our most popular contribution to world vocabulary: "OK." Openness and Kindness are what make life **OK.**

In every situation, resting in openness and acting with kindness is the right answer; the entire trick is to put yourself where these two intersect, and function at the junction. Like the egg and the chicken, openness and kindness give birth to one another in an endless circle. Being good really does help us get to heaven (within), while being in heaven helps us to be good.

BIG FRED

I used to have an upstairs neighbor, an old, overweight ex-boxer with bad knees, who worked as a janitor. Fred would generally come home with his groceries, a couple of six-packs, and a stack of lottery tickets while I was in the middle of my evening meditation; through my door I would hear his labored breathing and the clanking of his beer bottles as he struggled up the stairs. At first I tried to ignore it. Then, as the contradiction grew more embarrassing, came annoyance—I would jump up and help him, but resent the fact that my practice had once again been interrupted. Because I'm a slow learner, it took a few weeks before I realized, This *is* the practice. If I have to sit cross-legged on a cushion to experience boundlessness, that's a boundary. Hauling beer up the stairs is the meditation, and Big Fred is the teacher.

> The only thing you can do now, the only religious thing you can do, is act. Act for God, if you want to—what could be prettier?
>
> —J. D. SALINGER, *FRANNY AND ZOOEY*

3.

NOTICE THE
MOMENT

"The rule is, jam tomorrow, and jam yesterday—but never jam today."

"It must come sometimes to 'jam today,' " Alice objected.

"No, it can't," said the Queen. "It's jam every other day: today isn't any other day, you know."

—LEWIS CARROLL, *THROUGH THE LOOKING-GLASS*

The moment just before the car crash seems like an eternity—that's what people say. Perhaps it's because that moment, and every moment, *is* eternity . . . only, as the tires screech and we're pressed back into the seat, we're paying attention for a change. If you've been in such a crash (or a near miss), you probably still recall, even years later, not only the slow-motion approach of the other car but your view of the road through the windshield, the feel of the steering

45

wheel in your hands, the precise quality of the daylight or the on-coming headlights filtered through the dry or humid air.

Perhaps you remember your first kiss the same way, or the birth of your child, or the time you scored a big goal or basket. In each case, the *importance* of the moment rivets your attention, with a vivid clarity that somehow bursts through the fabric of time. What makes sex ecstatic is not only the intensity of physical sensation, but how that intensity makes us pay attention to what's happening *now*, makes the past and future melt away, awakening us to the ecstatic quality of timelessness. Music works in much the same way: a Ravi Shankar or Jimi Hendrix or Fritz Kreisler or Lester Young uses his instrument as a power tool to slice and dice time, leaving us in that space which, even if it's only a split second on the clock, lasts forever because it *is* forever—the underlying timeless silence revealed.

John Brown, as he was being carted off to be hanged for leading the raid at Harper's Ferry, was heard to say, "This *is* a beautiful country." We can imagine that at that moment, no longer consumed by apocalyptic visions of the nation's destiny or last-minute anxi-eties about his own, Brown was freed from agitation in time and could rest at last in the timeless clarity of the moment. But do we need to be on the gallows (or in the birthing room, or in a car crash) to achieve that kind of clarity? Must it be reserved for "important" moments? Or can we live outside time all the time?

TARGET PRACTICE

Here's an experiment. Starting from about a foot away, please bring your finger *very* slowly toward the target till it touches it. Repeat a few times, paying close attention to your experience, before reading on.

OK. This may sound silly, but did you notice that your finger is always exactly where it is—that it's never anywhere else? When the situation of being a foot away from the target exists, the situation of touching the target does not exist. When any intermediate position exists, none of the others exist.

Now, does the moment of touching the target have any more weighty reality, any more importance, than all the moments of not touching it? If so, where does that importance reside? In the finger? In the target? Or in your mind? Try it a few more times—play with the situation, get intimate with it.

The tricky part, you may notice, is the habit of dividing our experience into "important" and "unimportant" moments. The important ones are those in which we're closing in on some kind of target, sinking a putt or closing a deal or solving an equation, something desirable for us to pull toward; or else there's something undesirable for us to push away from, like a fight or a car crash. The rest we tend to ignore.

Each morning there's a time in the bathroom when I've turned on the shower and I'm just standing, waiting for the water to get hot. I'm eager to roar into the day, to get to the important moments, but there's nothing for me to do just then. I actually used to try to make that unimportant time disappear by mentally counting ("One Mississippi, two Mississippi, three Mississippi") to distract myself from having to consciously live through that nothing-happening time. But "nothing happening" is precisely where it all happens—where the mind rests in freedom. Trying to make the present moment go away is cutting yourself off from the time when you can glimpse the timeless.

As if you could kill time without injuring eternity.

—THOREAU

To embrace eternity instead, we can start by changing some of the habits we've developed to distract ourselves from it. Don't automatically turn on the radio every time you get in the car, don't turn on the TV the moment you find yourself home alone, don't read the newspaper every time you get on the exercise machine, don't light a cigarette or pick up a magazine every time you find yourself waiting. There *is* no waiting; there's only being.

On our journey through life, we think of, say, stopping for gas or going to the bathroom as time out from the main event, from our "real" activities. We think of the time we spend walking down the corridor from Office A to Office B as intermission, dead time, mere connective tissue. But there is no intermission. The show never stops. Every moment is the only moment.

> *There's nothing special about the present moment except that it's all we have.*
>
> —CHARLES GENOUD

Guy walks into a bar and sees a big sign: FREE BEER TOMORROW. So he comes back the next day and asks for his free beer. The bartender points to the sign and says, "Whatsa matter, buddy, can't you read? It says, 'Free Beer *Tomorrow.*'" It's never the future. It's never the past. The ancient Greeks had no idea they were ancient. They experienced themselves as living *now*, on the cutting edge of modernity, wearing the very latest styles in togas. And the Jetsons, or whoever lives in what we picture as the gee-whiz future, will also be living *now*. Back in the 60's or 70's, someone came up with the refreshing slogan, "Today is the first day of the rest of your life." But we can go further and claim our freedom from the future as well as the past by saying, "Now is the only moment of your life."

THE LENGTH OF NOW

Well then, if now is all we have, how long do we have it? Here's another experiment. Try saying the word "now" very, very slowly. Notice that first you say *n-n-n*, then *a-a-a* (as in "cat"), then *oo-oo-oo*.

N-N-N → A-A-A → OO-OO-OO

While you're saying *a-a-a*, where are the *n-n-n* and the *oo-oo-oo*? They have no reality then, just as finger-touching-the-target and finger-a-foot-away have no reality during the intermediate positions. And by the time you get to the *oo-oo-oo*, where have the *n-n-n* and the *a-a-a* gone?

> *Into the air, and what seem'd corporal*
> *Melted, as breath into the wind.*
>
> —*MACBETH*

If we say "now" really fast, does that change matters? It can speed up the appearing-and-vanishing act to the point where our ear is fooled, just as the magician's nimble fingers fool our eye, but even if we pronounce it in a nanosecond, it's too long: it's still a succession of nows, masquerading as *now*. No matter how fine we slice it, any amount of time is too gross to express the timelessness in which we actually live. The real now has no length at all.

Yet in the continuity of this timelessness, the events we call "time" somehow happen. From its mysterious center, the present perpetually blossoms. To experience this mystery, watch something in continuous motion, such as a stream or waterfall, or listen to a continuous sound, such as the roar of traffic on a busy street. Notice that you're always seeing or hearing precisely in the present, never even one second in the past or future, yet somehow you can experience the continuity. It's really quite baffling, yet we do it all the time.

NOTICE THE MOMENT

Time is the moving image of eternity.

—PLATO

So there is no sequence of moments. There's only one moment, which is perpetual, or, we could say, eternal. Many people assume that "eternity" means an unthinkably long time—all the zillions of years we can imagine plus a smidgen more. Similarly, they assume that "infinity" means unthinkably big—all the zillions of miles we can imagine, plus one more inch to completely boggle our minds (like the overstuffed stomach of the glutton in *Monty Python's The Meaning of Life:* "Just one wafer-thin mint," and ka-boom!). Infinity, however, is neither big nor small; it has nothing at all to do with space. And eternity is neither long nor short; it has nothing at all to do with time. This misunderstanding has provided material for many spectacular hellfire sermons:

> *What must it be, then, to bear the manifold tortures of hell for ever? . . . Now imagine a mountain of . . . sand, a million miles high, reaching from the earth to the farthest heavens, and a million miles broad, extending to remotest space, and a million miles in thickness: and imagine such an enormous mass of countless particles of sand multiplied as often as there are leaves in the forest, drops of water in the mighty ocean, feathers on birds, scales on fish, hairs on animals, atoms in the vast expanse of the air: and imagine that at the end of every million years a little bird came to that mountain and carried away in its beak a tiny grain of that sand. How many millions upon millions of centuries would pass before that bird had carried away even a square foot of that mountain, how many eons upon eons of ages before it had carried away all. Yet at the end of that immense*

stretch of time not even one instant of eternity could be said to have ended. At the end of all those billions and trillions of years eternity would have scarcely begun.

—JAMES JOYCE, *A PORTRAIT*

OF THE ARTIST AS A YOUNG MAN

Whew! This is ingenious but, fortunately, confused. Eternity is not zillions of years; it's the timelessness of now, in which there are *no* years.

FREE SPACE

The good news applies to this world as well. Twelve Step programs have the right idea with "One day at a time," but we can go further with "One moment at a time." Our habit is to blur one moment's problems into the next, to say, "My stomach hurt all day" or "He's constantly making fun of me." But if you pay close attention you'll see there are numerous mind-moments throughout the day when there's no stomachache or ridicule—great spaces of present freedom, untainted by past and future.

Sometimes this freedom practically ravishes us, if we let it. Where are your business problems when you sneeze? Where are your times tables at the moment of orgasm? (The "problem" of 9 x 12 exists only when we think about it.) Where are your religious conflicts and political confusions, or your broken heart or your tragic childhood, when the roller coaster is screaming down that first hill? We may be convinced we have to "process" and "resolve" our traumas before we can drop them, but in fact we drop them repeatedly. (And then pick them up again. Why?)

Living in nowness means living at ease. When we sit at that red light with our knuckles turning white on the steering wheel, isn't it because we're trying—impossibly—to strain forward into the future moment when the light will turn green? After an emotional confrontation, don't we mentally replay the conversation, trying to splice into the past what we now realize we woulda, coulda, shoulda said? Fortunately, you don't need to stop such habits. Simply notice that your thoughts about past and future are only thoughts and that you're always thinking them in the present. Then you're no longer lost in them, and that's the crucial difference.

So the past always only *was*, the future always only *will be*, the present alone *is*. We're the donkey. The future is the carrot dangling on the stick just ahead of us, the past is the pink ribbons of nostalgia and the clanking tin cans of trauma tied to our tail. Dreaming of beginnings and endings, we're always in the middle, and the beat goes on. Through the repeated practice of finding freedom in the space of present awareness, we awake to our situation and stop chasing the mirage of fulfillment outside the now. Then every meal is our last meal, every kiss our first kiss. Then we're living our life. As my wife says, "I hope you're having a good time, because *this is it*."

NOW WHAT?

Listen to the way people say, "Now what?"—usually in a sort of sarcastic huff, not as a lucid opening into this moment but as an irritated anticipation of the next (half holding their breath, tensing their muscles as they brace for calamity). But inflected differently, that same phrase can be the mantra that reminds you to notice the actuality of the present: the what of the now. Just breathe out and use the phrase as your cue for an innocent, wide-eyed, appreciative encounter with whatever the present presents. I used to dogsit a neighbor's sweet-tempered white Labrador retriever. Taking Butterbeans for a walk was always a wonderful lesson in "Now what?" Tongue out, tail wagging, she greeted each rock, tree, squirrel with total enthusiasm, then dismissed it and moved just as enthusiastically to the next.

Living in the present doesn't mean hedonistic irresponsibility about the future—shouting *"Carpe diem!"* as you fall drunk down the stairs and pretend there won't be consequences in the morning. Of course nowness doesn't abolish the sequence of cause and effect, but it radically shifts the way we experience it. Every time we look it's still now, but we go from now to now as if crossing a stream on stepping-stones; we must step alertly, with surefooted balance.

That also means not rushing. You can move quickly: rushing is not a fast physical speed but a harried mental state, one that blurs our vision as we strain to lean into the future and so miss the present. In fact, the clearer our sense of now, the faster we can move without getting lost in time-blur.

Festina lente. (Hurry slowly.)
—CAESAR AUGUSTUS

One way to develop this skill is through your posture. Start by watching pedestrians on a city sidewalk. You can usually pick out the ones who are rushing, not only by their speed but by the way they carry themselves: shoulders slightly hunched, head down, bent slightly forward at the waist as they lose themselves in thoughts of their destination and try to lean into the future where they've already arrived. Then practice walking in a nonrushing posture and notice that you can walk plenty fast this way: head up, shoulders back and down, looking about and enjoying the passing scenery instead of worrying about being late. (You're not late till you get there.)

MELTING MASKS

Time is of the essence—the essence of our sense of being a limited, wavelike identity defined by specific traits, rather than limitless ocean. Strictly speaking, there's no such thing as, say, a vegetarian or a Republican, only a pattern of behavior in past moments which may or may not be repeated in future moments. When we say, "He *is* a vegetarian," or "She *is* a Republican," we're using the present tense to blur past behavior into an illusion of solid, continuous, once-and-future reality.

> *It depends upon what the meaning of the word "is" is.*
> —BILL CLINTON

Certainly for practical purposes we must make such generalizations, but we shouldn't be too shocked when they break down, because they're not solid identities, only shifting patterns. The present, because it does not endure even for a nanosecond, is too short for us to "be" anyone or anything; in zero time there are no patterns.

If this sounds like an abstraction, here's an exercise that makes it more concrete. Go through your photo album and find pictures of yourself when you were younger. (Actually, they're *all* pictures of you when you were younger, including a Polaroid snapped one minute ago.) Look at yourself in infancy, in high school or college, with your old boyfriend or girlfriend, and so forth. Gazing at a picture, try to recall what it felt like to be "you" then. What preoccupied that person? What did she want? What was she worried about? What feelings dominated her life? Repeat this process with other pictures, and as you do, see if you can actually reinhabit each past state—can you *be* that person now? If not, where is the solid, continuous identity that supposedly runs through time?

In fact, the word "person" comes from the Greek *persona*, mask. Time is the glue that holds our masks together. The insubstantiality of time reveals the insubstantiality of everything we think we "are," of all those limited identities.

ACCEPTING THE PRESENT

The mystery, as it turns out, is not eternity, but this elusive thing called time. What *is* this strange mechanism that keeps turning the future, which we're never experiencing, into the past, which we're never experiencing? Even Einstein shrugged his shoulders and said time is that which clocks indicate.

To notice timelessness is to receive the gift of the now, to accept the present of the present. This moment is already however it is; it's too late to change it. Any striving to improve things can only be aimed at the future, even the future one second from now. That's a worthy occupation, but sometimes we need to take a vacation and abide in what *is*, now after now.

In time, everything becomes old and stale, but now is ever-fresh; it redeems the routine activity that civilization requires. Drudgery becomes freedom, a chance to melt into timelessness within the reliable structure of the routine. The same-old same-old becomes the same-old brand-new.

> *See, now is the acceptable time; see, now is the day of salvation!*
>
> —2 CORINTHIANS 6:2

4.

RECOGNIZE
TEACHERS

*There is no perfect teacher. . . . The point is to
make a sincere effort to become a perfect student
of an imperfect teacher.*

—ISSHO FUJITA

San Francisco in the fall of 1967 was a wonderland for spiritual explorers. The early, idealistic days of the so-called hippie movement had brought seekers from all over the world, and teachers were there to meet them. Suzuki-roshi taught at the Zen Center in Japantown, Swami Bhaktivedanta had opened a Hare Krishna temple in the Haight-Ashbury, Rabbi Shlomo Carlebach led his group of ecstatic young Hasidim, Sufi Sam taught spiritual dancing, Master Paul was training Christian mystics, and there was even an outfit called The Messiah's World Crusade that ate macrobiotic food and waited on Mt. Tamalpais for the flying saucers to land.

And today was registration day for the Experimental College, a program in the spirit of the times, which San Francisco State College sponsored. Card tables had been set up around the perimeter of the student lounge, each with a teacher or two to chat up prospective enrollees. And there I was, blond mane to my shoulders (also in the spirit of the times), moving from table to table like a nibbler at a smorgasbord, asking each teacher why I should take his or her course: the placid-eyed yoga lady, the Tarot couple in Egyptian robes, the young guy in the necktie teaching Transcendental Meditation, the two rival tai chi instructors (one of whom, clearly furious at the other, performed a short routine and challenged him to match it), the popular local psychedelic evangelist offering a seminar called "Magic, God, and Einstein."

One man sat quietly at his table, his fingers laced together, behind a small, hand-penned placard reading DICK COHEN, ZEN MASTER. He looked to be in his mid-30's, with short (for that era) curly brown hair, sport jacket, and open-collared shirt. He was about the least remarkable looking person in the room. In spite (or perhaps because) of that, I found myself interested; besides, I had read a little about Zen koans and liked the pun of his last name. "So," I said, planting myself in front of him, "tell me why I should study with you."

He remained motionless, his fingers still laced together. "Oh," he said, "you don't want to study with *me*."

This intrigued me. "I don't? Why don't I?"

He gave me a knowing wink, nodded his head gravely, and said, "*You* know."

I had no idea what he was talking about. But between his conspiratorial tone, my reluctance to confess ignorance of any kind, and the sudden pressure of the moment, I found myself returning his slow, knowing nod. Unfortunately, he responded by nodding *again,* compelling *me* to nod again in return, upon which *he* continued to nod, and then there we were, like a pair of those perpetual-motion toy birds that keep dipping their beaks in the little cup of water, stuck in a mutual nodding loop with no way out.

Suddenly he stopped in mid-nod and shook his head once, quickly, from side to side. It was like the screeching of brakes. Paralyzed, I had no idea what to do or think. My ego and intellect short-circuited, I felt naked, defenseless—which was, of course, right where he wanted me. "You see?" he said. "You need the yes *and* the no."

That was the end of my training with Dick Cohen, Zen Master. I never saw him again. I signed up for a couple of less scary courses, which turned out to be largely forgettable, but I'm still learning from that awkward one-minute encounter. His yes-and-no has proved to apply to just about everything in my life, including all my further dealings with teachers.

FIRST TEACHERS

Do teachers have the answers? Yes and no. Whether their field is bowling or enlightenment (or both), they save us from having to discover all knowledge from scratch in each generation. Yet we can't just take their word for everything, but must confirm it through our own experience and refine and expand upon it. You can't have Einstein without Newton, but you can't have Einstein without looking *beyond* Newton.

Are our teachers easy to recognize? Yes and no. Not all teachers have formal status as coaches, professors, priests, rabbis, or Zen masters. They may be friends, enemies, lovers, animals, rocks, trees, jobs, situations, illnesses, even characters in books; the big bird in *David and the Phoenix* shaped my life more than most of my school-teachers. They can be the accidental teachers who teach by negative example—whose patterns of confusion show us what to avoid. We can be deeply grateful to such people for suffering so that we may be free.

Precisely because we have so many teachers in the course of a lifetime, it's important to credit them for what they have taught us, whether in sweetness or hardship, through yes or through no. It's said that the worst thing you can do in a job interview is to dis your former boss. Someone who spends his life noisily resenting his ex-spouse or -lover or his last year's friends makes *this* year's friends wonder what he'll be saying about them *next* year. The great Jewish wisdom book *The Ethics of the Elders* says that a person is your teacher if he teaches you just one thing, no matter what else happens between you.

This is especially important with regard to our first teachers—our parents. The Ten Commandments offer a surprising health tip:

> *Honor your father and your mother so that your days*
> *may be long in the land.*

In Eastern cultures, veneration of parents is considered vital to health and prosperity, but here's the same concept of filial piety in the "Western" Bible, implying some kind of subtle karmic dynamics. What are they?

Through your parents you're connected to the whole amazing

phenomenon of life as it grows and replicates in time: living forms emerging from emptiness, Russian dolls within dolls, the linking of past, present, and future in the magical chain of DNA. By relating with positivity ("honor") to the link closest to you ("your father and your mother"), you connect positively to the whole chain, and the whole chain naturally resonates with positivity. That means you create a harmonious relationship with the environment ("the land") and so naturally thrive there ("your days may be long").

In more down-to-earth terms, you are in many inescapable ways (genetically, attitudinally) the extension of your parents. *You're made out of them.* As long as you're at war with your parents, you're at war with yourself, with your own body and mind, grinding your gears, generating stress that shortens your days in the land. Were your parents imperfect? Get over it—so were everyone else's. Honoring them doesn't mean adopting all their values or condoning all their actions. But even if they abandoned you or abused you, they gave you this body; they are the gate through which you entered this life.

Honoring your parents means thanking them for this gift. You can honor them to their faces through a hundred small, inadequate gestures of kindness and respect. From a distance, you can include them in your practice of exchanging self for others, putting yourself in their shoes as they went through whatever they went through to raise you. You can take a moment every day to mentally thank them for your ability to draw the next breath and hear the next sound. Then, even after death has delocalized them, your relationship can continue and ascend to ever higher levels.

THE HEAVY ONES

The most exalted form of teacher is the enlightened spiritual master, the sage, the guru. Do we really believe in such people? No and
yes. In our culture, the word "guru" is often used as a joke, or de-
valued to mean a mere technical expert ("He's our Macintosh
guru") or even something sinister and Svengali-like (I once heard a
respected PBS interviewer say, "You've been accused of being a
guru"). Perhaps this shouldn't be so surprising when "mantra" has
been reduced to mean a vapid political slogan and "Om" is a
cologne. At the same time, I think we suspect and hope that "guru"
still means something authentic that defies trivialization. Related to
the word "gravity," it signifies someone who's *heavy* where the rest of
us are lite, who has the gravitas to be grounded, as immovably as a
rock, in the unchanging nature of reality, even as the rest of us are
blown about like dry leaves.

Of course there's no shortage of cranks and charlatans, but
there are also people who *seem* to be the genuine article—certainly
such heavyweights of the past as Jesus, Socrates, the Buddha, Saint
Teresa of Avila, Machig Labdron, the Ba'al Shem Tov, and Pad-
masambhava. And nowadays, rather than rely on books or rumors,
many students can have direct contact with heavy teachers.

But some misconceptions are still common, such as the idea that
working with a guru means relinquishing all independent thought,
or that teachers are one to a customer. In some Asian cultures one
might call a dozen people "my guru." Every teacher, as he or she
points toward infinity, stands in a slightly different place; the spot
on the horizon where all those pointing fingers converge is where we

want to go. True, mixing teachings can be tricky. My friend Ed used to practice with a Zen group, where one meditates for long periods sitting absolutely still. Enduring pain can actually become a bit of a macho competition, but at least at the end of a session everyone gets up off their cushions slowly as they recover the feeling in their legs. One weekend, Ed attended a retreat run by Tibetan Buddhists, who are much more relaxed about how they sit—they'll shift their position, scratch themselves, even have a drink of water. During the first session, Ed, who is a burly guy, thought, "I'll show *them* how to sit!" and maintained his Zen-style immobility. Everything was fine till the session ended and everyone stood up quickly. Ed tried to jump up with them—and fell flat on his face.

The main confusion, however, stems from a fundamental misunderstanding of the nature of enlightenment. Existence has two aspects: *samsara*, which can be roughly defined as life's normal craziness, and *nirvana*, which is boundless, indescribable freedom. The misconception is that enlightenment means going from A to B, when in fact it means realizing that A and B are never separate.

The fool seeks nirvana and tries to get rid of samsara.
— LONGCHENPA

Gurus embody this state of affairs. They're like some kind of cosmic candy bar: nutty samsara on the outside, creamy-smooth nirvana on the inside. Their experience of textureless, superfluid freedom gracefully coexists with all the textures and bumps that make humans human—talents and limitations, likes and dislikes, cultural biases, wacky personalities. But that's good news: if the gurus are human like us, then we're potentially enlightened like them. In fact, the most skillful ones make a point of leaving their bumpy human individuality undisguised, so that their students don't waste time trying to iron out their own bumps.

Traditionally, the guru is associated with the moon, which reflects the light of realization symbolized by the sun. It's an apt metaphor. The teacher lights our way through the dark night when we can't see the infinite ourselves. Yes, the moon is always reflecting the sun's light. No, because of its phases it's not always reflecting it in a direction that we can see. Gurus, like the moon, can put us through a lot of changes in the process of reflecting the changeless. Sometimes dealing with them is like having cookies and hot chocolate with Grandma; sometimes it is, as Chögyam Trungpa Rinpoche put it, like having surgery without anesthesia. I've had the same teacher answer my most thoughtful questions patiently and encouragingly or give them a dismissive brush-off. I've had a teacher privately yell at me about how stupid I was (true in that case) and five minutes later present his most cherubic countenance to an audience of two thousand. Yes, they can give us what we need; no, they don't act the way we think they should.

In the 70's, one wonderful white-bearded pundit from India—who looked like most people's image of God the Father, wrapped in an orange robe—started coming to retreats in Europe, where he gave learned discourses on the Rig Veda, Hinduism's most ancient scripture. In the evenings this great religious scholar would hang around the kitchen and retrieve empty yogurt containers from the trash, as if they were rare treasures. Intrigued, a friend of mine who worked on the kitchen staff finally peeked into the pundit's room. There he saw hundreds of carefully washed yogurt containers stacked in a giant, floor-to-ceiling pyramid. Anything's possible. We try to make rules for these characters, but their nature is to defy our rules—they're too big for us to wrap our concepts around.

NOT IN KANSAS

Probably the best movie on this topic is *The Wizard of Oz*. Dorothy, the Scarecrow, the Tin Man, and the Cowardly Lion set out on the Yellow Brick Road like seekers on the path to enlightenment. Determined to find the sage who, rumor has it, can solve all their problems, they head for the Emerald City of Oz. (Lhasa? Jerusalem? When Dorothy asks for directions, the Scarecrow points east *and* west.) Once they arrive, Dorothy's three friends ask the Wizard for brains, heart, and courage, precisely the goals of understanding, love, and self-confidence that motivate most people to seek teachers. Dorothy, however, asks for something more profound: a way *home*, that is, a way back to her source, her original nature, nirvana.

Does the Wizard grant these boons? Yes and no. The things that Dorothy's friends seek, being aspects of the kingdom of heaven, are within them. The teacher can't give you anything you don't already have, but he can put you in situations that bring it forth. (The word "education" comes from a root meaning "to draw out.") So the Wizard pits them against the Wicked Witch of the West, and in the process they are forced to manifest the brains, heart, and courage they had all along.

And, oddly enough, Dorothy was home all along. As the film ends, it looks as if the Wizard is going to take her back to Kansas in his balloon, just the way we'd all like to hitch a ride to enlightenment and let the guru drive. But something's missing—her dog—and as the balloon floats away she jumps out, refusing to leave without him. ("Toto" means "all," and evidently Dorothy's bodhisattva commitment won't let her enter nirvana until she can take all beings with her.) Fortunately, she has only been dreaming she's lost in Oz, just as we dream we are lost in samsara. To wake up (the literal meaning of "buddha"), she merely has to chant the mantra that acknowledges the omnipresence of nirvana throughout samsara. "There's no place like home"—literally—because home is not a place. It's everyplace. When you're awake, there's no place *but* home.

By then Dorothy has also discovered that the Great and Powerful Oz is just a fraudulent little man behind a curtain. His exalted status is a product of thrones and microphones and smoke machines, like the intimidating pomp and pageantry of religions. He's just a kindly, bumbling carnival flimflam artist whom Dorothy has dreamed into a wizard. And yet his methods work. Apparently a dream wizard is the perfect solution to a dream problem.

HOW TO LEARN

So, if we were to compile a list of practical guidelines for dealing with teachers, the first might be: don't be shocked when you discover that they're human. (Early Christianity wisely declared it a heresy to deny that Christ had human qualities.) Idealizing the teacher is dangerous. It's usually followed by disillusionment when the teacher fails to conform to a model that is our own creation, not his. Fine, he's got feet of clay, but it's pointless (and bad manners) to dwell on it. Pay no attention to that man behind the curtain.

The second guideline might be to listen carefully—pay *close* attention to what the man behind the curtain *says*. I've been in situations where, an hour after a lama's discourse, the students remember diametrically opposed versions of what he said. It makes you wonder what can happen to a teacher's words after a few thousand years.

The third guideline would be, having clearly heard the teacher's words, to act on them. Reading the books and attending the seminars is a good place to start, but if you don't go home and practice, you're expecting the teacher to do all the driving. The teachings may or may not be precious wisdom in a form that you can personally put to good use, but the only way you'll ever know is to try them out. (Be a good scientist.) If the teacher says to turn right, turn right and see what happens. And if the next day she says to turn left, you can either complain that she's contradicting herself or else assume, till it's proven otherwise, that she's guiding you through the twisting paths of your own mind.

STORMY WEATHER

To keep following directions through all those twists and turns requires some degree of commitment. Committing to a teacher or a tradition of teaching is like fastening your seatbelt; being strapped in allows you to speed along faster and go safely through bumpier, scarier terrain. It doesn't require some kind of fierce emotion or absolute conviction. If you sometimes wonder whether the teacher knows what he's doing, that's OK. It's a standard part of the drama—there's some yes and no to it. The Gospel of Mark has a lovely allegory on this point:

> On that day, when evening had come, [Jesus] said to them, "Let us go across to the other side." And leaving the crowd behind, they took him with them in the boat, just as he was. Other boats were with him. A great windstorm arose, and the waves beat into the boat, so that the boat was already being swamped. But he was in the stern, asleep on the cushion; and they woke him up and said to him, "Teacher, do you not care that we are perishing?" He woke up and rebuked the wind, and said to the sea, "Peace! Be still!" Then the wind ceased and there was a dead calm.
>
> —MARK 4:35–39

Here we have all the elements of the teacher-student dynamic. A teacher extends an invitation to "go across to the other side," to the far shore of realization, the kingdom within. A group of students leaves behind the uncommitted masses (the crowd) and joins the teacher in the vehicle of the teaching (the boat). Significantly, the teacher goes "just as he was," with all his human frailties (apparently exhausted, non-Superman that he is, from a full day of teaching and being jostled by crowds). And while Jesus instigates the trip, like the Wizard, he doesn't just take the students where they're going; they have to sail the boat themselves and face some challenges on their own.

The windstorm, like most supernatural stories, is much more interesting if we read it metaphorically. Anyone who has gone on a journey of commitment—rehab, marriage, a theatrical production, a season on a sports team, a meditation retreat—has been through that windstorm: the part where the going gets rough, you're convinced that all is lost, and the rehab counselor or spouse or director or coach or guru appears to be snoozing on the job. But then (if she really is a guru) she works her magic and calms everything down, mainly by calming every*body* down; for the real storm is inside us, as is the nirvanic "dead calm" that follows it when we realize that everything is under control.

ATTACK OF THE CHATTERING CHAMBERMAIDS

On a long retreat, where you're pretty well deprived of external stimuli, this drama is often played out in its most purely psychological—and sometimes comical—form. I studied for several years with Maharishi Mahesh Yogi. One of the many practice slogans that he drummed into us till we could recite them in our sleep was, "Noise is no obstacle to meditation." On a winter retreat in an off-season beach hotel on the Mediterranean island of Mallorca, I was sitting in my room, dressed in long underwear and wrapped in a blanket, meditating for up to six hours at a stretch. (Don't try this at home.) Across the hall was an alcove where the chambermaids, who seemed to have a lot of time on their hands, would congregate and gossip. Unfortunately, I understood just enough Spanish so that my mind could keep itself nice and busy, alternately translating and seething.

Surely Maharishi didn't mean that *this* kind of intrusive noise was no obstacle! Surely Maharishi was asleep at the wheel if he was allowing such unacceptable conditions to persist—I'd best take matters into my own hands. A few times, therefore, I jumped up, stormed out the door, and shouted at the maids, but the sight of me in my long johns, sputtering with rage in bad Spanish, only made them laugh. Finally I complained to the retreat manager, who somehow convinced the maids to gossip elsewhere.

Now I could practice—except that now, in the absence of the maids' voices, I found myself distracted by the intolerable hissing and gurgling of my radiator. I piled heavy books on it to damp out the vibration. I tried different settings on the control knob. I moved my seat around the room in search of elusive acoustical dead spots. At last I found the delicate combination that reduced the noise to just below my threshold of hearing. *Now* I could practice—except that now I found myself listening to the sound of the waves, incessantly lapping up on the beach. Maybe I could ask Maharishi to do something about it. . . . That's when I realized, "No, wait. We live in a world of noise. I can fight it and go insane, or I can accept it and decide that—*aha!*—noise is no obstacle to meditation!"

This is called skillful teaching. Maybe Maharishi or Jesus really could stretch out his hand and make the waves subside. Who knows? But what would that accomplish? The real miracle is that, by holding fast to a teaching, we can subdue the storms of our own minds.

MINGLING

One practice that works with the student-teacher relationship at its deepest, most potent level is called *guru yoga* in Sanskrit, *lama'i naljor* in Tibetan, and Holy Communion in Catholicism—opening to infinite reality through the intermediary of the teacher. Guru yoga is often described as mingling one's mind with the teacher's mind, or we might say we're locating the radiant spaciousness of the guru's being and finding it identical to our own.

> *Jesus said, "Whoever drinks from my mouth will become like me; I myself shall become that person, and the hidden things will be revealed to that person."*
>
> —THE GOSPEL OF THOMAS

Some traditions do this through formal rituals or elaborate visualizations; some use simpler, more emotion-driven approaches (singing the gospel hymn or *bhajan,* letting Jesus or Lord Ram into your heart). Simpler still is this stripped-down, essentialized version:

Sitting relaxed with eyes closed, think of your enlightenment-teacher—whoever for you at this time most clearly embodies limitless awareness and compassion. Whether you have met in the flesh or even lived in the same century doesn't matter. It's good if you feel some connection with the teacher, although that will develop with practice. You can even imagine a hypothetical guru. In any case, don't worry about details. Rather than try to visualize the teacher, allow yourself to feel her presence, her most subtle essence, that which makes her what she is. (It may have some flavor of clear, brilliant light.) Notice how it surrounds you and pervades you. Then just rest your awareness in that—settle into it as into a warm bath. Whenever your mind wanders off, gently bring it back and continue to soak, letting the thoughts melt into that subtle, radiant presence.

The walking-around form of this practice is to recognize everything and everyone as the teacher. Guru yoga works because what a
realized teacher has realized is pure being, independent of any form,
which is the ultimate nature of *all* forms, wherever they may be in
time or space. The teacher is nirvana shining through samsara, and
that's all we ever meet.

> *Maybe you think that a teacher has a body or bones or*
> *hair. . . . That's the relative teacher. . . . Truth is every*
> *single momentary arising, the entire phenomenal uni-*
> *verse. The absolute guru or teacher is the nature of all*
> *things. Don't think it is just some old man, some lama*
> *or guru figure.*
>
> —NYOSHUL KHENPO RINPOCHE

At this level, there's only one teacher, whether you call it Life or
Christ or Vajra Guru or Whatchamacallit. Therefore the trees and
stars you see as you walk your dog, and the dog and the leash and
the sidewalk and you, are all of the teacher's nature. Just recognize
every sight and sound as the teacher's way of saying hello.

> *I am here and I am in America. Whoever remembers me,*
> *I go to.*
>
> —NEEM KAROLI BABA

This technique should never become a strained, artificial mood or
complicated concept. The nature of the teacher just *is* and needs no
help from our emotions or intellect. Just rest in it, steep in it, dissolve into it.

In time, you can practice guru yoga in the most challenging situations, seeing the sullen supermarket checkout clerk, the incompetent minivan driver blocking your lane, the telemarketer who interrupts your dinner as the teacher in various masks. You can see problems and illnesses as the teacher instructing through tough love. Eventually every situation, even the most disastrous, becomes not a matter of "Why is this happening to me?" but "What is my teacher teaching me?" And it all takes place within that warm bathtub, where whatever confronts you in each moment confers the experience of infinity.

Usually we get just glimpses of this infinity, but sometimes even a glimpse can change everything. One day on a street in Florence when he was nine years old, Dante glimpsed it shining through the face of Beatrice, and it inspired a lifetime of ecstatic poetry. The young monk Ikkyu, while drifting across a lake one night in a rowboat, heard it in the cawing of a crow; that sparked his enlightenment, and he went on to become one of Japan's most illustrious Zen masters. But you don't have to be a 13th-century poet or a 15th-century monk—you're surrounded by such teachers if you can just recognize them.

> *The Awakened Ones always joyously teach and indicate with every word and wordless gesture the absolute inexhaustibility of pure presence.*
>
> —PRAJNAPARAMITA SUTRA

CATCHING THE TRAIN

One morning I found myself running through the Newark, New Jersey, train station, trying to make a connection to New York, dodging frantically through the crowd as complex scenarios of missed appointments flashed through my mind. I reached the steep stairway to the platform and ran up, two steps at a time. Blocking my path at the top was a heavy swinging door with a large, grimy window set into it; on the other side an old man in faded work clothes was washing the glass with a spray bottle and rag. Out of the middle of the grime he had just wiped a clean circle about a foot across, through which, our noses inches apart, we now faced each other. Suddenly all the worry and hurry in which I had been caught up seemed to be illuminated in the morning light breaking through the circle, and then to drop away. It was as if the window were my clouded mind and the old man with his rag had made a clear space for me to see, once again, that everything was light, everything was fine, and it always would be.

Am I making too much of a simple encounter? (Did Dante?) I don't know . . . maybe . . . yes and no. All I know is that the old man smiled broadly, and in that moment I could have sworn he knew exactly what he had done. Then he opened the door for me and stepped aside as the train pulled into the station.

5.

KEEP IT
SIMPLE

I always listen for what I can leave out.

—MILES DAVIS

Life is basically pretty simple. You get up in the morning, you do the things you have to do, and if you have time you do some things you want to do. You try not to hurt people and you help them if you can. Then you go to bed.

We can, however, make it very complicated. There's no straight line that can't be made crooked, no easy task that can't be made hard, no clear statement that can't be obscured, no ordinary encounter that can't be twisted into ingenious and endless ramifications. Even Victor Serebriakoff, former president of the brainiac society Mensa, once said, "Unfortunately, intelligence is no guarantee against stupidity."

But there's a direct path out of all these needless entanglements, a simple way back to simplicity. In our life, as in Miles's music, the trick is to listen for what to leave out. And in Miles's spare, muted playing in, say, "All Blues" or "Stella by Starlight," you can hear what richness can be coaxed out of the silence if you leave out enough. You can also see it in the evolution of film acting, from the melodramatic gesticulations of the 20's to today's intimate, stripped-down style, where the actor can say everything with a subtle shift of his gaze. After working with Robert De Niro, Quentin Tarantino observed that, while most actors try to impress a director with how many different ways they can play a scene, De Niro's genius lies in seeing that there are only two or three valid things you can do in a situation—and knowing which ones they are. That's the deal: suss out what needs to be done, do it with a minimum of wasted motion, and move on.

We don't have to get lost in a dizzying array of choices. The 13th-century monk-philosopher William of Ockham gave Miles's slogan a more technical shape: "*Entia non sunt multiplicanda præter necessitate.* Entities should not be multiplied unnecessarily." Now considered an essential tool of scientific method, this formula—Ockham's Razor—cuts through all needlessly complex explanations of a given set of data and, till proven otherwise, assumes the simplest explanation to be true. In the same way, we can cut through all needlessly complex responses to a given life experience and, till proven otherwise, assume the simplest response to be best.

A saint is a very simple man:
when he walks, he walks,
when he talks, he talks,
and that's all.

—SUJATA

Here's one of the neatest writing tricks I know; I discovered it while I was working as a film critic. Let's say I've created a monster sentence like this:

> *A distinct majority of the population of the United States appears to derive a sense of pleasurable diversion from direct engagement in the act of collectively witnessing displays of commercial entertainment belonging to the cinematic mode.*

First I turn the page over or look away from the computer screen, forcing myself to visually disengage from the tangle of my own words. Then I ask myself, "What are you trying to say?"

Usually the answer comes as a simple declarative sentence. "Oh, I'm just trying to say, 'Most Americans like movies.'"

"Then say *that*. Quick—write it down!"

Sometimes our lives can seem like that sentence: a wearying tangle of needless complication, sound and fury signifying nothing, or, to use the technical term, samsara. With the sword of discernment (a close cousin of Ockham's Razor), we cut through the tangled jungle of samsara and find the clear, open space of nirvana—or at least a little clearing in the jungle. Sometimes it's as easy as looking away from whatever you're snagged in and asking yourself, "What are you trying to do?"

Often what keeps us tangled is too much thinking. One Christmas morning I found myself sitting on the living room floor, surrounded by the pieces of a new gadget with "some assembly required," scratching my head over the instructions. As my son walked by, he paused, scooped everything up, ignored the instructions, said,

"Look, this goes here and that goes there," and in a flash it was done. How did he know? As the artist Peter Delman says, "You see and you know." Between seeing and knowing, I was interposing too much thinking.

FEEL YOUR FEELINGS

Some people make things complicated by filling journals with long, convoluted entries, recording not only the events of their lives but their feelings about the events, and their feelings about having those feelings, and other people's feelings about those feelings, and . . . Part of the problem is confusion about what feelings actually are. As the word implies, they're something you *feel,* an essentially physical sensation. If you're walking past an alleyway and someone jumps out and shouts "Boo!," a feeling of shock or surprise runs through your body. A moment later you might start to tell yourself a mental story about it: "I feel that it was rude for him to shout that way," or "I feel that it was like the horrible shock I suffered on my fifth birthday when I was traumatized by that scary clown." But now you're not really discussing feelings but thoughts *about* feelings.

Feelings are spontaneous, are just *there,* and are therefore simple. Our stories about them are as complicated as we make them. So one way to keep our lives simple is to cut through the stories and come back to the feelings—feel them raw and direct, not filtered through a sieve of thoughts. Before, in response to the "Boo!" we might have felt a powerful wave of anger or fear welling up and thought we needed to put some kind of brake on it. So we might have suppressed it, which is painful because it requires a lot of inner clenching and grinding to bottle up the feeling somewhere in the body. In fact, past experiences of painful suppression are precisely what have convinced us that feelings are painful and need to be suppressed.

Instead we can apply a procedure recommended in Tibetan teachings, as summarized by Ngak'chang Rinpoche: "Let it flood." Anger, grief, joy, surprise, feelings we can't even name—whatever's there, take a moment to drop everything else and let it be there, without judgment, fully experiencing the richness of its flavor. At the same time, don't fixate. Rest in openness to whatever appears, including your feelings. The breeze from the electric fan is there, the sound of the ice cream truck is there, the anger or joy is there . . . and the wider context, the skylike nature of mind itself, is always there, bigger than any clouds of feeling that might drift across it.

Letting your feelings flood doesn't mean sloshing them onto others. (What you do with others is be kind. One of the many rewards of acting with kindness is that it helps keep life simple; one of the many punishments of cruelty and thoughtlessness is that they make life incredibly complicated.) This is strictly an internal affair, not a reckless process of acting out. In fact, by finally allowing yourself to feel your feelings till they've run their course, you'll probably find that the urge to act them out, along with the compulsion to analyze them ad infinitum, has evaporated. And fully experiencing "negative" feelings frees up the capacity to experience "positive" feelings as well. Eventually we find that they're neither positive nor negative; they're just feelings, in the same way that all colors are just colors. Rage is just rage, as in a raging storm, a force of nature, which blows for awhile and then is gone. "Positive" and "negative" are superimposed stories.

*There is nothing either good or bad, but thinking makes
it so.*

—*HAMLET*

The wisdom of this traditional teaching has been confirmed by medical science. One clinician, Dr. John Sarno, has discovered that, in an effort to distract themselves from suppressed feelings, people commonly generate psychogenic pain, especially in the back—a logical place to put things we don't want to see. The pain is physically real, but its origin is purely a game of emotional hide-and-seek, even when the MRI shows herniated discs; studies show that about two-thirds of the general population are walking around pain-free with herniated discs and don't know it. Working with thousands of patients suffering from long-term chronic pain, Dr. Sarno has found that, by simply acknowledging the underlying feelings instead of focusing on the physical symptoms, they can break out of the cycle of pain and anxiety, often within days. (I wouldn't have believed it either if I hadn't seen this work for a close family member and a couple of skeptical M.D.s.)

MARRIAGE MADE SIMPLE

Our personal relationships can also be simpler than we usually make them. Whether in a romance or a marriage or a family, the principles are the same: you take care of one another, you be as kind as you can, you do your share of finding new sources of fun, you quietly pass up opportunities to score points or be a wise guy, you give the benefit of the doubt, and you try to make things less insane rather than more.

You're either part of the solution or part of the problem.

—ELDRIDGE CLEAVER

If you think the other person is off the program you address the situation gently and with respect. But since the problem is often in your own perception, you can save everyone a lot of grief by waiting a little while first to see if your perception changes.

My friend Peggy has been married for more than twenty years:

At first there was some butting of heads as we tried to figure each other out. Over time, it became easier, less effort, more of a natural flow. I think the key for me was learning to see what's not important—which is most of it—and being willing to talk about the rest. If the other person is at all reasonable, they'll usually go along. For example, I've always been extremely punctual. My husband is always late; it seems to be in his genetic makeup. When I realized this was a battle I couldn't win, I gave up being punctual. I had to make the decision to bicker my whole life or let it go. And there wasn't a sense of, "Well, now he owes me one." In fact, it turned out to be better for me. I discovered that it was OK to relax and arrive at 8:05 instead of 8:00.

The more things you let go of, the simpler it gets. Not every couple figures this out—my in-laws never did. They loved each other madly, but they spent their lives having big battles over little things, like which way to cut the carrots. It's just not worth it.

WHEN IN DOUBT, BREATHE IN, BREATHE OUT

It's easier to *keep* things simple than to *make* them simple. When my father used to take me sailing, he would hand me my slicker and say, "It's easier to *stay* dry than to *get* dry." But most of us keep finding ourselves wet again and need ways to dry off. Think of your life as a big, noisy game of Monopoly. In the heat of playing you can get completely wrapped up in whether you'll get that hotel built on Marvin Gardens before the top hat gets out of jail, or whether you can advance your thimble to Go without having to pay rent on Park Place. Then there's a clap of thunder outside. You look up, and for a moment the reality of the game dissolves into a wider reality. When you return to the game, its grip on you has loosened a bit— you can feel some of the space around it.

When such thunderclaps as heart attacks or house fires strike our lives, we often realize how trivial and gamelike our usual, complex preoccupations are. But why wait for the thunder? Look up and see if, just for a moment, you can drop everything.

Or else *breathe* into the simple actuality of the moment. Sometimes you may feel as if you're drowning in complexity. To keep from drowning, you may be unconsciously holding your breath. Instead, let go of that constrictedness, along with everything else. Draw the next breath, freely and with full attention, and then let it out. That breath is always simpler than whatever else is going on, and powerfully grounding: a few conscious breaths can reconnect you to the simple concreteness of the body and, in turn, to your immediate surroundings and to their simplest, most pressing needs.

Then respond to those needs in direct, straightforward ways. Fix the leak, weed the garden, change the diaper, pay the bills, feed the hungry. Deal with the present, which is far simpler than constantly sorting through the past and the future. Let the complexity of mental stories and worries resolve into the simplicity of physical action. It's matter over mind. The unlived life is not worth examining.

UNCLUTTERING

We can also reduce complexity by reducing clutter. Most people have a closet (or a drawer, or a house) full of old papers that have lost their relevance, mementos that have lost their charm, and the wreckage of discarded projects and outgrown interests. Everything that's stashed in the dark recesses of that closet has a corresponding place in the recesses of your mind. In *Walden,* Thoreau recommends an occasional ritual burning of such old junk. Once a year I get together with a few friends in a clearing in the woods for a Henry David Thoreau Memorial Purificatory Bonfire. Everybody has to bring one item, preferably one that's not too easy to let go of. As we take turns around the circle, Little League certificates, unfinished manuscripts, photos of old girlfriends, and letters from old boyfriends are displayed and explained before being chucked into the fire. Sometimes tears of relief are shed. (If the stuff might be useful to someone else, you can give it away or donate it to the Salvation Army.)

Thoreau, of course, is the American patron saint of simplicity, whose experimental sojourn in the woods reduced life to "the Four Necessaries": food, shelter, clothing, and fuel. He was suspicious of the high tech of his day—the railroad and telegraph—and from the grave casts a cold eye on all our electronic bread makers and computerized kitty litter boxes. Me, I love my credit card–sized voice recorder and my wristwatch gizmo that remembers phone numbers and appointments; by letting me forget about stuff till I need it, they help me keep my mind clear. But technology's tricky. It's easy to drown in e-mail or become the pager's slave instead of its master. Thoreau invites us to look afresh at each gadget and ask if it really redeems its own clutter:

> *We are in great haste to construct a magnetic telegraph*
> *from Maine to Texas, but Maine and Texas, it may be,*
> *have nothing important to communicate.*

In that spirit he would certainly recommend that you kill your cell phone, or at least save it for dire emergencies. Before its advent, the car and the train were among our last havens of incommunicado quietude. Commuting time could be silent communing time, and somehow we got along fine.

The ultimate clutter casualty is the hero of what is usually considered the greatest American film: *Citizen Kane*, the story of the compulsively acquisitive tycoon who dies, alone and bitter, in his fabulous castle Xanadu, uttering the mysterious name "Rosebud." After a reporter's fruitless quest to discover what Kane was calling out for—what the man who had everything lacked—we see Kane's cavernous basement, stuffed with more treasures than he could unpack in a lifetime. In the final shot, an oblivious workman tosses Kane's childhood sled, bearing the name "Rosebud," into the furnace, along with other discarded junk.

Kane is usually viewed as a cautionary tale, depicting the greedy materialist's loss of innocent childhood happiness. Fair enough, but that overlooks the real irony of the ending. Kane's problem was not that he lost his Rosebud. He had it all along, but his life was cluttered with so much other stuff that he couldn't see it. In the same way, we can never lose the pure, simple being that is our very nature. No amount of surface complexity can destroy that deep simplicity, but it can keep us from seeing it—till we learn to look through the surface into the depths. Kane just needed to check the basement.

So we don't have to toss all our stuff and move to a cabin on Walden Pond after all. Thoreau's motto of "Simplify! Simplify!" is valid only up to a point. We don't have to *make* life simple; it's always already simple, even on the busiest day in the most hectic metropolis. We just have to keep noticing the ocean and then live the waves in that context. "Simple" therefore doesn't mean simplistic or simpleminded. True simplicity doesn't need to annihilate richness and complexity; it can handle commitment and responsibility.

A FIELD TRIP

For another kind of lesson in being simple, let's take a trip to the old folks' home. As we walk down the corridors, we can see every stage of the process we'll go through ourselves, quickly or slowly, as we approach the end of life: the falling away of complicated circumstances, of tricky intellect, of tangled explanations. We may get ten years of Alzheimer's or two seconds after the truck hits us, but ready or not, simplicity will be our only option. So our sense of who we are, what is what, and how we know had all better be simple.

*Only mature minds can grasp the simple truth in all
its nakedness.*

—RAMANA MAHARSHI

When we see old people who have lost their sexuality, their homes and possessions, their futures and pasts, it generally shakes us up, but when the saints and buddhas relinquish these same things we venerate them. Maybe that's because we think we're more likely to get old than to become saints. But the enforced simplicity of old age is a great opportunity if we know how to embrace it. With luck, we may stay active and alert right up to the end. Just in case we reach a point where our main occupation is sitting, however, it's good to have had some practice. Then, when everything else melts down, if simple, unfixated, open awareness is left, we're fine. Spend enough time in the old folks' home and you'll discover that the residents keep asking two questions: "Where am I?" and "What am I supposed to do now?" The correct answers, which can make our last years a time of serenity rather than confusion, are "Right here" and "Just be."

When I've forgotten how to quote Shakespeare and argue politics, I intend to remember how to sit and just be. (We'll see!) If I can no longer navigate the horizontal logic of coherent conversation, I can still sink vertically: if I can only babble I can happily babble the Hail Mary or the Mantra of Great Compassion. In case the exit process happens quickly, I'll have to revert to my practice without time to go over my notes. When Gandhi was shot, he called out the name of Rama—his preferred name for the infinite—before hitting the ground. That's the final exam, and, no matter when or how it comes, it's always a pop quiz.

THE NATURAL STATE

The simplest way to learn those answers down to your bones is to rest in openness. That's the ultimate simplicity, where, if you're doing anything, you're doing too much. Buddhists say "Preserve the natural state," which is a pretty close paraphrase of KEEP IT SIMPLE. Not *construct* the natural state— it can't be constructed because it's already present. As we come to see that we have been superimposing complexity onto simple reality, we naturally stop doing that and complexity dissolves like snow falling on water.

A Zen story:

Three friends are walking along a country road. They see a man standing on top of a nearby hill. The first friend says, "He must be standing on top of the hill to look for his straying cattle."

The second one says, "No, I think he's standing on top of the hill to find his lost traveling companion."

The third says, "Perhaps he's standing on top of the hill to enjoy this pleasant breeze."

Unable to agree, they climb the hill and ask the man, "Are you standing on top of this hill to look for your cattle, to find your companion, or to enjoy the pleasant breeze?"

He replies, "No. I'm just standing on top of this hill."

6.

BE DEVOTED

It's better to see God in everything than to try to figure it out.

—NEEM KAROLI BABA

You're gonna have to serve somebody.

—BOB DYLAN

And they got married and lived . . . happily . . . ever . . . after.

That's right. All their troubles came to an end, and together they ascended to a state of unbroken happiness so perfect that it went on *forever*.

Wow!

It was lovely to believe in that kind of ending to things—once upon a time, a long time ago. But then we grew up, and the term "fairy tale" came to mean a cozy lie. The adult equivalent, in which Prince Charming and Cinderella have morphed into the likes of Hugh Grant and Julia Roberts, bears the almost equally derogatory name of "chick flick." And yet . . . even if it's a lie on the literal level, could it be an intuitive metaphor for something that's true on a deeper level—some transformative process that really can elevate us to a state of happiness beyond time?

In the fairy tale, kissing the frog or saying "I love you" to the beast lifts the spell; he becomes once again a handsome prince, which turns out to have been his true identity all along. Kissing Snow White or Sleeping Beauty awakens her from her deathlike sleep, to ride off with the handsome prince to a shining castle in the clouds. The insinuation is that any beastliness or unconsciousness we may have fallen into is not our real nature, but some kind of bad dream or spell, and that some specially focused, exalted form of love could have the power to break the spell, wake us up, reveal our true identity, and transport us to a heavenly kingdom. The same spiritual traditions that say there is such a kingdom (within you) also say there is such a love: devotion.

> *Among things conducive to liberation, devotion alone holds the supreme place. The seeking after one's real nature is designated as devotion.*
>
> —SHANKARACHARYA

Our impulse toward devotion, I suspect, is so deeply ingrained that we all look for objects toward which to direct it. We're built for it the way birds are built for flight; without millions of devotees, neither Beatlemania nor the Roman Republic could have happened. So the question is not *whether* but to *what* or *whom* you will be devoted. By harnessing our natural tendency toward devotion and pointing it toward an appropriate object, we can put it to the service of liberation. We can kiss the frog of warty, flawed existence, freeing it—and ourselves—from the spell.

This is not merely an emotional or attitudinal shift, but a perceptual transformation. When I was ten years old I was a devoted coin collector and experienced this in a small way. Pennies, the most worthless of coins, began to reveal a greater value and beauty. Through my focused enthusiasm (love) for them, I literally started to see aspects I hadn't seen before: this one was in Extremely Fine condition because all the lines in the wheat stalks were clear and sharp, that one was rare because it had the designer's initials (V.D.B.) on the reverse. My enhanced perception of the coins in turn fed my love for them, which further enhanced my perception, which in turn fed my love . . .

In this way devotion becomes self-perpetuating. If you just stay with it, keep opening to the same object, your appreciation grows without limit. You may have experienced this with your children, your country, your work, your art. If you're a devoted musician, you hear subtleties of rhythm and timbre that other people don't; if you're an artist, you keep seeing light, shapes, and colors in new, vivid ways; if you're a fly fisherman, you know things about the river that can't be put into words.

In principle, it doesn't matter what the object of devotion is. If we focus steadfastly on any wave it will eventually be revealed as ocean. But in practice, we have to choose a wave whose form and color attract us so we'll stay focused. (Unlike coins, stamps never turned me on.) In the case of romantic devotion that means, depending on what's important to you, you might have to be with the person whose sparkling eyes or shapely figure, funky humor or political passion, artistic power or earning power entices you. We don't love our lovers *for* those qualities, but, initially at least, we love them *through* those qualities.

BREAKFAST WITH
THE INFINITE

Since devotion eventually requires steadfast commitment to one object, romantic devotion goes all the way in a situation called marriage.

> *Kneeling 'neath your ceiling*
> *Yes I guess I'll be here for awhile.*
>
> —BOB DYLAN

The procedure is simple. If you worship (that is, acknowledge) your partner as the infinite, then you get to set up house with the infinite, eat breakfast with the infinite, make love to the infinite. Such worship doesn't require you to relate in an artificial or saccharine way; that would just confuse the issue. You relate in a way that's natural and ordinary because devotion is the gradual discovery that the natural and ordinary is the infinite. It doesn't require you to prostrate yourself at her feet (although that might be an interesting exercise). It doesn't require you to suppress your occasional anger or other "negative" feelings, which are a natural, ordinary feature of relationships, or to idealize her charms and virtues, which are irrelevant to her status.

It's all much bigger and quieter than that. She is the goddess, he is the god, the finite embodiment of the infinite, not by being wonderful but by *being*. Serene or irate, gorgeous or homely, young or old, clever or slow—with sufficient devotion, none of this finally matters. Whether your mate worships you in return also doesn't matter. All that is required of the devotee is to be there, in the face of whatever the beloved presents, kneeling 'neath her ceiling. Instead of fantasizing about the person of our dreams, we devote ourselves to a *real* person and so awaken. "Hopelessly devoted to you," sang Olivia Newton-John in *Grease:* devotion means giving up all hope that the beloved will be this way or things will turn out that way. As in all spiritual practices, just be steadfastly wide open, without expectation or judgment. In short: surrender.

True, most spouses need some feedback so they can learn and grow too. The line between devotion and codependency can be thin. But that's one of the things that makes this a process of wide-awakeness and not creamy-dreaminess. If he's messing up you need to tell him (and if he's abusive you need to dump him). The trick is to deal with the problem on the active surface level of the relationship while continuing to accept and worship at the silent depth. Think of Ralph Kramden in *The Honeymooners,* who, even in the midst of his ranting—"One day, Alice! Bang! Zoom!"—always knows deep down, as he declares in the final embrace, "Baby, you're the greatest!"

PITFALLS

The opposite of this "Beauty and the Beast" approach is seen in Nathaniel Hawthorne's short story "The Birthmark," in which a scientist grows obsessed with the tiny discoloration on his otherwise "perfect" wife's left cheek; the potions he brews to remove it wind up killing her. The effort to impose perfection on the surface, rather than recognize it at the depth, usually results in some kind of destruction. Carried to its logical extreme, it becomes the fascist requirement that everyone be uniformly straight and healthy and beautiful according to some theoretical ideal or else be eliminated. The antidote to fascism is humanism, which not only tolerates but glories in the quirks and splotches that make us unique. Carried to *its* logical extreme, it becomes the devotion that reveals everyone to be worthy of worship. When you've seen one wave to be gleaming ocean, by implication so are all the others.

There are other pitfalls on this path of romantic devotion. One is the notion that living with your god or goddess must always be a matter of *intensity*. We may have experiences of romantic and/or sexual fireworks, especially early on, then spend our lives trying to sustain or reignite them. But if we look closely, we'll see that fireworks per se are not what's so gratifying—it's the spaciousness, the luminous clarity that's left after the fireworks blow away our constrictions of heart and mind, and *that* we can have in ever-stronger doses.

Addiction to intensity has led countless people to pursue disastrous relationships and to wreck or pass up healthy ones. But intensity is only the booster rocket—trying to fire it continually leads to burnout. It's needed initially to attain escape velocity, but once you're cruising through deep space you switch the booster off. Then things get very quiet: you're not going to hear that roar or feel that G-force. *But that's fine.* Even though it may feel as if nothing is happening, you're actually traveling much faster now. And once you recover from the blinding flash and your eyes adjust, you'll notice that deep space is illuminated by steady, brilliant, silent starlight, billions of times more dazzling than any rocket fire.

STRONG STUFF

In this context we can reconsider the Commandment "You shall not commit adultery," not as a finite restriction but as a way into infinite freedom. We've got to focus on our one and only if we're going to perceive her as The One and Only, and sexual energy is too powerful not to affect our focus.

> *With one tookhes [behind] you can't dance at two weddings.*
>
> —YIDDISH PROVERB

Sure, monogamy presents its own problems. Like democracy, it's the worst possible system except for all the others. (Of course, for the Old Testament Hebrews, who practiced polygamy and concubinage, this Commandment had nothing to do with monogamy.) In general, women seem to be psychophysiologically more wired for monogamy. Men—this is no secret—seem to be wired to spread their seed as wide as possible. So conflict, and therefore drama, is built into the system. But the news, gentlemen, is that, as in the chick flick, for this drama to have a happy ending the woman must win.

Certainly life is complicated. It's far too simplistic to say that every romantic encounter not sanctioned by a lifetime contract wreaks nothing but damage; it might be an act of great tenderness and caring, or at least a harmless roll in the hay. In youth especially, a certain amount of exploring and fumbling about is standard. The term "adultery" applies to adults. Once we've reached a certain level of maturity, we know that unconditional commitment opens the heart, and that life with a closed heart is not worth living. Sex is not dirty, shameful, or of the devil, but it's strong stuff, and if engaged in with inappropriate persons it creates chaos. Who's inappropriate? If you're an adult, you know.

But sometimes you feel attraction to others besides your partner? OK. Rest in that. Desires are just desires—not every desire has to be fulfilled. We've learned how to let feelings be, without suppressing or acting out; this frees us from the tired routine of oscillating between guilt and lust, like Goofy being jerked back and forth between the Goofy angel on his right shoulder and the Goofy devil on his left. Besides, the impulse to physically merge with those others loses much of its urgent edge when you're *already* merged with them on the level of ultimate identity: you don't need to unite your wave with that of each passing babe when, with growing clarity, you experience that you and she are already one ocean.

Firmly committing to one partner under all circumstances (in sickness and in health, come rain or come shine) is like setting a camera on a tripod. It provides the steadiness necessary for a long exposure, which, even in near darkness, eventually produces a clear view, awash with light. See what develops: the camera of awareness records the true face of the partner, which is also our own true face and the face of existence itself. And in this way, love not only stays alive over the many years of a marriage, but flourishes. As awareness gets clearer, love gets deeper—turns out, in fact, to be bottomless.

Such a process deserves, if anything does, the label "sacred." This is what those who condemn marriage between two people of the "wrong" gender or color or religion fail to grasp. Whatever reveals the infinite is sacred, and any union based on devotion does just that.

KRISHNA BLUES

Like romantic devotion, religious devotion requires steady focus on an object. HaShem or Jesus, Mary or Vishnu, Allah or Yeshe Tsog-yal . . . pick a deity, any deity. Again, the crucial element is your affinity for it, your ability to open to it, and that may be conditioned by any number of factors, including family traditions and karmic proclivities. If you felt that affinity, you could pick up the next bubble gum wrapper you found on the sidewalk, put it on your desk, and keep coming back to it day after day to worship it as the infinite.

Does that sound like idolatry? Isn't there a Commandment against that? It's idolatry if the gum wrapper remains a mere gum wrapper. Our strategy is to use the idol to go beyond the idol. The Commandment against bowing down to idols, or "graven images" in the older translations, emphasizes that the problem is fixing your veneration on anything limited and rigid, as if etched in stone. The most rigid images can be the ones graven in our minds, our fixed ideas of the way things are; the way things *really* are is bigger than our ideas. If *we're* rigid enough we can turn anything into a frozen idol, including, say, the Bible, or Commandments carved in a rock, or a bearded deity who carves them.

I had my first taste of this process in my hippie days, circa 1967, hanging around the Hare Krishna temple in San Francisco. The temple was actually a converted storefront a few blocks from Haight Street, whose walls were covered with oversized paintings of scenes from the life of Lord Krishna—God in the form of a beautiful blue-skinned youth who wanders through the countryside, strolling through fields of flowers, herding cows and charming the milkmaids with the sound of his flute. At the far end of the room was a small curtain that opened to reveal a shrine filled with garlands, incense, food offerings, and, yes, idols.

But in chatting with the devotees (white robes, shaved heads, ponytails) and doing some reading, I learned that this apparently primitive, pagan, idolatrous stuff had very sophisticated implications. The flute song of Krishna represents the seductive call of the infinite, wafting through the finite world. We are the milkmaids, who, sooner or later, one way or another, are seduced and open ourselves to receive the infinite as a woman receives a lover. And Krishna is blue because the sky is blue. That is, the sky is colorless (and formless, and endless), but to us it *looks* blue. So Krishna, or any other object of worship, is a form of the formless, with names and stories and attributes that give us a way to connect with it and eventually fathom its essential nature, which has *no* attributes.

Not I, not I, but the wind that blows through me!
—D. H. LAWRENCE

A devotional practice you may want to try, then, is to sit before a picture or statue of a favorite saint or chosen deity, what Hindus would call your *ishta-devata*. Relax alertly, and softly gaze into her eyes. Don't stare, don't try to feel holy, don't try to feel anything in particular—whatever happens happens. Just be there and give up. Then give up some more.

Why bother with the picture at all? You may not need to. It depends on how much form you feel you need at a given time. If the blue of Krishna represents the blue of the sky, why not just gaze into the sky? As a matter of fact, that's now one of my favorite practices.

THE MAGIC SPOON

When my father was a boy in Brooklyn, the local merchants used to sell a product called the Magic Spoon. Aluminum pots were popular then, but cooking certain foods turned their insides black. Housewives were advised to fill the pot with water, put in the Magic Spoon, add a pinch of cream of tartar from their spice rack, bring it all to a boil, and (like magic!) the pot looked brand-new. The scam, of course, was that the spoon did nothing—cream of tartar is the active ingredient. All religious images, idols, rituals, rosaries, phylacteries, mantras, and messiahs may be Magic Spoons. No problem, if they're the catalyst that will get you to apply the real active ingredient, your own awareness, in the prolonged boiling action of devotion. Jesus makes this clear when he says, "Why do you call me good? No one is good but God alone"—he has no unique value of his own, but is only a conduit for the infinite value. (That's no small thing.)

If Jesus or Krishna or Tara or the Blessed Virgin happens to be a conduit to which you connect, that's wonderful. If, though, you find that you're not getting any juice—that you're just sitting through services that are boring and lifeless (for you)—you may want to shop around. These days you can stroll into a good bookstore and read your way from Anabaptists to Zoroastrianism, or go online and download everything from digitized Sufi songs to animated Vajrayana prayer wheels. Or else you can stay with the old conduit but enhance your ability to draw from it by applying all the skills we've been discussing: resting in openness, being in the moment, and so forth. You can stay right where you are, doing all your old practices, only finding in them a new, ever-deepening resonance. Then, instead of the hymns and sermons being merely a pleasant dream of a promised future—another fairy tale—they start to be a description of the experiential present.

Remember to be a good scientist. This is all lab work. If you can keep the pot boiling without some kind of Magic Spoon to catalyze the process, so much the simpler. Otherwise, choose some form of the formless that appeals to you. Find some way to bow down to it with your body, with your mind, with your heart. Invent your own practices if you prefer. You don't have to get fancy; in fact, that can be a distraction.

That's another thing I learned about in the Krishna temple. The services there consisted mainly of chanting:

HARE KRISHNA, HARE KRISHNA,
KRISHNA KRISHNA, HARE HARE,
HARE RAMA, HARE RAMA,
RAMA RAMA, HARE HARE.

Often the temple would be filled wall-to-wall with devotees, hippies, an occasional college professor or tourist, and other assorted drop-ins. Some people would do a simple dance step with arms upraised toward the altar, some clapped their hands or played finger cymbals to a simple beat (one-two-*three*, one-two-*three*), while a few banged on traditional drums or blew conch shells as the chanting built to a climax. Then came the "love feast": delicious (and free!) Indian food, a bonus for those with no visible means of support.

One day a guy with a big, shaggy brown beard comes in lugging a conga drum. He's *very* good. As the chanting gradually accelerates, he improvises more and more intricate rhythmic figures and exquisitely inventive fills. It's one of the most amazing musical experiences I've ever had. Midway through the service, one of the devotees sits down next to him with his own drum and says, "No, like *this*." Boom-boom-*boom*, boom-boom-*boom*—the same crude, simple beat as the hand claps and finger cymbals. I'm surprised and angry at first, but eventually I get it. It's not about performing. Even if you're your own audience of one, if you focus on the intricacy and aesthetic beauty of the devotional process, you miss the point. Do just enough to connect with the object, let go, and fly into its heart.

WORDS OF POWER

In fact, chanting is one of the most powerful of devotional practices because it's one of the simplest. It can be done anytime—walking, driving, exercising, working in the yard, when you can't sleep, or at the beginning or end of a sitting session. You can use any prayer or mantra. You can sing it, say it, mutter it, think it, or let it glimmer and dissolve into the space beyond thought. You can sound it in a continuous stream, or, like a gong, sound it once, let it reverberate in the space of your awareness, and then sound it again. Just start it however you feel it at the moment and let it flow. Don't try to make anything happen; go along for the ride. (A hardcore method is, at the end of a hot shower, to suddenly turn the water to cold and then, as it streams onto the top of your head, *yell* the mantra.)

Physically, the sound vibration helps massage the body into a state of alert relaxation. As you repeat the words, you may sometimes feel engaged with their meaning, sometimes with the sound beyond the meaning, and sometimes with the presence or actuality beyond the sound, which is what the meaning was about all along. But all that takes care of itself. What's important is to let go and throw yourself into it. Don't approach it as a bunch of repetitions to slog through. Fully inhabit each syllable, as if it's the last thing you'll ever do, as if it's the note you'll ride out into infinity—which, in that present moment, it is.

Here are a few more vehicles that have been extensively test-driven. All translations are inherently inadequate.

- DAYENU
  It would have been enough. (Whatever we've already been given is perfect—the rest is gravy.)
- GATÉ GATÉ PARAGATÉ PARASAMGATÉ BODHI SVAHA
  Gone, gone, supremely gone, supremely totally gone, awake—yippee!
- GOD
  (The word with which many people have the deepest connection, the one that evokes most vividly their aspirations to the ultimate, and the one they involuntarily blurt out at moments of crisis.)
- HARI OM NAMO SHIVA
  Hail, great destroyer of ignorance.
- LA ILAHA ILLALLAH
  There is no infinite but the infinite.

- MM-HMM
  Fine, OK, that's the way it is, I accept it.
- MOST SACRED HEART OF JESUS, HAVE MERCY ON US
- MOTHER OF MERCY, PRAY FOR US
- NAMAHA
  I bow down.
- OM AH HŪNG
  (Untranslatable cosmic sounds—can be used separately or together.)
- OM AH HŪNG BENZA GURU PEMA SIDDHI HŪNG
  Om ah hūng; diamondlike teacher who is always in the lotus of my heart, enlighten me; hūng.
- OM MANI PADME HŪNG
  Om, the jewel is in the lotus, hūng. (See page 140.)
- SHEMA YISROEL, ADONAI ELOHENU, ADONAI ECHOD
  Hear O Israel, the Lord our God, the Lord is one. (Open your awareness, you who have wrestled with the ultimate, and experience that the nature of boundless being and the nature of the world of boundaries are one: nirvana is samsara.)

WE DREAM OF GENIES

To practice devotion you don't have to believe anything. Jesus, Buddha, and the rest of the advance scouts in our explorers' club are not dictating beliefs; they're extending a jolly invitation. They're beholding the staggering beauty of creation, the all-grief-shattering perfection of each moment, and, just as amazed as anyone else, proclaiming: "Whoa, check *this* out!" They're way too busy enjoying the kingdom of nirvana to care what you believe.

Faith is something else again. Remember the overwhelming feeling, when you were a child, of knowing you were "in trouble," as if a giant weight had been rolled upon your heart? And notice how laughably weightless that same trouble seems now? Faith is not belief that someone is going to miraculously take away your problems, but the confidence (based on growing experience) that, from a larger, truer perspective, your problems are weightless—not just that everything will turn out all right, but that, even if you can't see it yet, everything *is* all right. People often turn to faith when, say, they fall seriously ill, but if you define faith as belief that God won't let you die, you're playing a game that you must eventually lose. Deep faith is trusting that somehow it's fine to live and fine to die—that the nonidentical twin frogs of living and dying are both guises of the same prince.

It's only human, when you're in desperate straits, to call out for help. But it's a more workable strategy if you also widen out your prayer to embrace the bigger picture. Jesus the role model showed how to do this when, facing his own death, he prayed, "Father, if you are willing, remove this cup from me," but then added, "yet not my will but yours be done." I often see NBA teams praying before a game and giving thanks to God after a win. Do they offer equally heartfelt thanks when they lose? I'd like to think that God is a Knicks fan like me, but if everyone prays to win, half of all prayers must be denied. Equating faith with the granting of your desires makes it a tool of the ego and reduces God to a servant with super powers, a genie in a lamp. Real faith and devotion bow to that which is bigger than the ego and supremely indifferent to its demands. If you don't worship something higher than your own desires, what's going to free you from *that* prison?

DEDICATED TO THE
ONE I LOVE

Perhaps the highest form of devotion is that which dispenses with all overt devotional forms and embraces everything we do.

> *Perform every action with your heart fixed on the supreme Lord.*
>
> —BHAGAVAD GITA

To do this authentically, to have your heart—your inmost core—fixed on the infinite, is a gradual, delicate process. The most effective approach is *service,* which combines the openhearted appreciation of devotion with the razor-sharp alertness necessary to see that our action is useful. This doesn't mean you have to think about God while you wash the potatoes; rather, wash them with full appreciation and attention, and the infinite shines *through* the potatoes.

Parents learn about service because children, more so than potatoes, demand to be handled lovingly, even when it's a dirty job. There's a story about Yasoda, the mother of Krishna, who as a little boy was particularly mischievous. One day Krishna's brother tells Yasoda that Krishna has been eating mud. Seeing it smeared all over his face and body, she orders him to open wide so she can scoop the mud out of his mouth—just a mom doing her job. But to her surprise, inside Krishna's mouth Yasoda sees the entire resplendent universe: the stars and galaxies, the elements of nature, all of time and space. Of course it's really *her*—her awareness—that has opened wide. We often say that for parents their own children are the whole world, and here we see how far that can go.

So, in the context of the most mundane tasks, devoted service gives us glimpses of the infinite nature of the finite. These glimpses come unbidden, right in the unglamorous world of mud and spit (and coffee grounds and antifreeze and Kaopectate). That's precisely why they feed our faith and keep us on the path. Even if the glimpse of the prince within the frog lasts only half a second, it shows us that that's his true, deep-down nature—beyond appearances, beyond time, happily ever after.

7.

NO APPOINTMENT, NO DISAPPOINTMENT

For nothing is ever what you expect it will be, nor is it quite like anything else.

—JOYCE CAROL OATES

Ever walk down a flight of stairs, arrive at what you think is the bottom, and then, as you step into space, discover that there's one more step? There's nothing wrong with either the stairs or our ability to walk, yet the clash between expectation and actuality can produce a rude shock.

Scrawl it on your wall with spray paint, scribble it on your mirror with lipstick, tattoo it on the insides of your eyelids: No Appointment, No Disappointment. If you don't build your world on expectations, it doesn't collapse when things turn out different. This is not resignation but liberation. It's disillusionment in the best sense: cutting free from the illusions that have bound us. And since all our expectations are based on what has gone before, it's opening up to amazing possibilities, to that which we don't know how to expect.

Expectation may be our most deep-rooted habit. Each moment is like the mail: you hope for that check from Publishers Clearing House, but you get what you get. And one thing that you usually get is yet another sweepstakes entry, so you can start hoping all over again. Life always promises that the check is in the mail. And the flip side of hope is fear.

Cowards die many times before their deaths;
The valiant never taste of death but once.

—*JULIUS CAESAR*

Even knowing this, it's easy to get lost in fearful expectation, suffering the emotional wear and tear of the 999 futures that won't happen, along with the one that will. Hope and fear, it's true, are only human. We don't have to suppress or banish them, but we can also touch down on the ground of actuality, the place beyond hope and fear which is always right here, the reality that is never moved by our hopes or fears no matter how much *we* are.

Every spiritual tradition has ways of doing this. Muslims may end any statement of their intentions with *"Inshallah*—God willing." There's not only a charming humility but a sensible pragmatism in acknowledging that even our cleverest plans are only plans. We build models of the future in our minds, but the actual world has a mind of its own.

DROPPING ASSUMPTIONS

Dza Patrul Rinpoche, Tibet's illustrious 19th-century vagabond lama, recommended a potent exercise for undercutting expectation. Every time you leave your home or town or loved one, or anything else to which you're attached, assume you'll never see it again. If that's too daunting you can at least drop the assumption that you *will* see it again. One of these times you won't; then, if you haven't been cultivating expectation full-time, it won't come as such a shock.

This may sound like a bleak outlook, but it's actually just the opposite. My friend Maureen fell critically ill one winter when she was a teenager; the doctors didn't think she would live to see the spring. She recovered, and when she saw the forsythia bloom she realized that each day or year she lived from that point on was, as she says, "all cream," and never to be taken for granted. Now she takes the blooming of the forsythia every spring as her personal reminder of this. So we can continue to leave people with a cheery "See you later" while mentally adding a footnote: "Maybe." This deeper truth sets us free—it evicts us from our cozy little cottage in Tomorrowland only to show us the limitless vista of Today. No longer distracted by coming attractions, we stop missing the main feature.

Again, there's nothing mournful about this state of affairs. In fact, it's very close to the root of laughter. Humor works largely by blowing away our expectations. We expect a whooping cowboy to ride a bucking bronco, but in *Dr. Strangelove* Slim Pickens rides a hydrogen bomb; we expect a detective to be deft and clever, but in *The Pink Panther* Peter Sellers is bumbling and obtuse; we expect a man to eat steak and wear shoes, but in *The Gold Rush* Chaplin eats a shoe as if it were a steak. Expectations blown, our minds are left momentarily empty and open, a state so essentially delightful that it makes us laugh.

There's also a deeper truth to Patrul Rinpoche's exercise. Because everything is always changing, the spouse we join for supper is not the same one we kissed good-bye at breakfast. So actually, every time we leave her we *are* seeing her for the last time. This realization gives people space to grow, to be born again—and again and again. It frees us into seeing their fresh presence, rather than freezing them into stale memories and concepts.

> *real*
>
> *eyes*
>
> *don't*
>
> *conceptual*
>
> *lies*
>
> —BERNARD GUNTHER

Does No Appointment mean we can't plan to attend a party next week? No, go right ahead; just notice that you plan *for* the future but you plan *in* the present. And know that the festivities you're planning may or may not happen. Actually, they *won't* happen exactly the way you plan, since planning is a process of estimation, an imperfect conceptualization of a later moment. Sometimes (flat tire, no party) our estimate is way off, and at some point (coronary thrombosis, no pulse) it breaks down completely. Precisely to the degree that we've been caught up in expectation, this is a big surprise. And to the degree that we're open to the richness of the moment, whether it meets our expectations or not, sometimes the flat tire turns out to be the most interesting part of the evening.

All this applies as well to the criteria we expect others to fulfill. Your criteria are part of *you*. Everyone else is *someone else*. The two will *never* correspond. Encountering that simple fact again and again is what makes having other people in your life an adventure, a challenge, and an exhilarating opportunity to see your expectations shattered and scattered. Your kids can grow up knowing that life is not like a tough math problem with one right answer—yours—but more like a big, clean piece of drawing paper that comes with a deluxe set of crayons. They can grow up happy and sane, knowing that they're loved unconditionally, not contingent on their making the varsity team or getting into Princeton.

Many people, lacking such parents, have a deep-seated unease that is a major obstacle to relaxing into the infinite. So religions always supply someone who *does* love us unconditionally. A very healing exercise is to just sit quietly, open wide, and allow yourself to receive that unconditional love from, say, the Blessed Virgin or Jesus, God or Kuan-yin or Chenrezig, or from the unnamed enlightened ones, whoever and wherever in time and space they may be. Even the most hardened of us can grant that in all the history of the universe there may have been at least one such Unknown Lover, who for at least one moment sent out an impulse of all-embracing affection, and we can let it engulf and soften us.

LIFE AS JAZZ

The ability to let go of expectation is also at the root of creativity. The poet John Keats called it "negative capability":

> . . . *that is, when a man is capable of being in uncertainties, mysteries, doubts, without any irritable reaching after fact and reason.*

Never knowing when or from what direction inspiration will strike, we can train to be loose yet alert, so we're always ready for anything. Archimedes' "Eureka!" discovery came while lolling in the bath. Visionary breakthroughs from *Frankenstein* to Fellini films to the structure of the DNA molecule have come out of dreams. Apples fall every day, but Newton was open enough to see a universe of implications in an apple's fall; stars shine every night, but van Gogh was open enough to see how they set the sky spinning with pinwheels of glowing color.

Obviously, negative capability is where jazz comes from; playing in that space of no plans is what makes it perpetually exciting and fresh. I play a little saxophone, and my friend Sean, who's a fine trumpeter, once gave me some advice about improvising: "You think of something . . . and then you don't do it." At its best, jazz is anything-possible open awareness made audible. But we could say that anything (playing hockey, making love, teaching math) becomes jazz if you do it this way.

> *Jazz in its purest form is just the mind connecting with itself.*
> —HOAGY CARMICHAEL

And when the mind connects with itself, what it finds is freedom.

JUST LOOKING

I have learned some dramatic lessons on this point from a remarkable teacher named Charles Genoud, a soft-spoken French-Swiss with a droll sense of humor and the sturdy, compact build of a former soccer player. An expert on Tibetan temple art and meditative techniques, Charles leads tours, workshops, and retreats all over the world. His specialty is a system called Gesture of Awareness, which introduces the experience of openness not through verbal teachings or silent sitting but through what he calls "useless actions"—such simple gestures as slowly raising and lowering an arm, touching another person's shoulder, or taking a single step.

In one exercise, each student picks a spot across the room and walks toward it. After a few repetitions, Charles interrupts them halfway to their goal and has them walk to a different spot instead. Then he invites them to consider: if we never reach the original goal, in what sense were we ever walking toward it? Where did that "toward" exist? Once we realize that it exists only as a mentally fabricated appointment, we start to see how many other kinds of "towards" we project. In our minds, we're always going somewhere; in actuality, we always *are* somewhere. When we're driving to work, "to work" is just an appointment. We're actually driving *here* (up the winding hill), and then *here* (past the little white church), and then *here* (stopped at the light next to that nice old T-bird). Eventually we may get to work; the odds are pretty good. But in the meantime, our experience of driving can open to *here*, liberated from narrow fixation on *to*.

About a week into one of Charles's retreats, I woke up early one morning and wanted to check the time so I'd know whether to roll over and go back to sleep. I was staying in a small, spartan room without a clock or nightstand and had left my watch on the floor beside the bed. Groping around for it in the dark, I felt myself growing frustrated. Suddenly a phrase flashed through my mind: *"Not looking to be finding—just looking to be looking."*

When people speak of a life-changing experience, it's usually something spectacular like battling cancer or climbing a mountain. Mine was this quiet realization—that I could move my hand around till it bumped into the watch or didn't, while my mind remained disentangled from any appointment with finding or disappointment at not finding. This discovery transforms the texture of every action in every moment. Our awareness gets unsnarled, turned right side out, freed into open-ended reality, the clear blue sky where we do what we have to do now and we're blissfully ignorant of what will happen next.

> *Whosoever surrendereth his purpose to Allah while doing good, he verily hath grasped the firm handhold. Unto Allah belongeth the sequel of all things.*
>
> —THE KORAN

DARE TO BE USELESS

To see how this transformation works on a fundamental level, stand awhile on one foot. Notice the feeling of tension and imbalance, and how the mind seeks resolution in the future moment when you expect to put your other foot down. But rather than get sucked into that seeking, rest in the experience of the unbalanced present, tension and all. After awhile, put the foot down and rest in *that* situation.

Or sit, close your eyes, inhale deeply, and don't exhale. Don't "hold the breath" in the usual strained sense of waiting to exhale— just relax and be completely in the world of held breath, where the world of out-breath doesn't even exist. Then breathe out and rest completely in *that* world. If you go on like this for awhile, you'll notice that, while you're in the world of held breath, you feel as if you could stay there forever. Resting in the timeless present, you're liberated from your appointment with future time.

Then . . . do everything like that!

You can start with activities that don't require a lot of thought. They're an ideal opportunity to practice resting in each step of performance as a "useless action," not a useful intermediate step leading to a next step. As you wash the lettuce, you're just washing lettuce; as you dry the lettuce, you're drying lettuce; then you're tearing the lettuce into the salad bowl; then you're picking up the knife; then you're slicing the tomato; then you're slicing the other tomato. Inhabit each moment of each activity as an end in itself, rather than a means to the end we call a salad. Then, if and when a moment arrives when you're eating salad, enjoy and inhabit that too.

Morning is the time when habitual patterns of worry and anticipation usually start to kick in. You can break out of them by starting the day like this, going through your morning routine in the spirit of uselessness: sitting up in bed, putting on your bathrobe, walking down the hallway, entering the bathroom, picking up the toothbrush, and so forth, letting each action just be that action, a world unto itself. In the world of shampoo-in-hair, the world of rinsing-shampoo-out-of-hair does not exist. This opens up a little space of nonexpectancy that tends to carry over, even as you encounter the more involving activities of the day; with practice, that space gets bigger. If you do the same as you prepare for bed, your mind will feel lighter, freer, ready for untroubled sleep.

During the day you can occasionally shift, even for one or two seconds, into slow motion—so you have time to perceive that reaching for the doorknob, grasping the doorknob, turning the doorknob, and swinging open the door are all actions in themselves, separate from each other and from the act of entering the room. Later you'll be able to do that without slowing down.

Whenever you find yourself temporarily cold or hungry or otherwise uncomfortable, rather than lose yourself in an appointment with future comfort, you can find great freedom by relaxing within the discomfort. Still, sometimes you will be engrossed in appointments, and that's OK too. Then you can learn by observing yourself. When my brothers and I were little, we would often come home from a family outing and race for the bathroom. While the winner relieved himself at his leisure, outside the door the other two would shift anxiously from one foot to the other, doing what in our family came to be called the Pee-Pee Dance. As people anticipate tomorrow's monster project or next week's confusing exam or Saturday's hot party, they spend a lot of energy doing variations of the Pee-Pee Dance. That's fine, as long as you know that all you're doing is dancing, and it won't open the bathroom door one second sooner.

There's never a reason not to relax.

—KEDAR HARRIS

THE SUBTLEST COMMANDMENT

There is fine insight into the wisdom of No APPOINTMENT, No DISAPPOINTMENT in the Commandment "You shall not covet." This instruction to give up envious desire is the most purely internal of all the Commandments, comparable to the Buddha's advice to give up attachment, the source of all suffering. And just as the Buddha listed Right Meditation last in the Noble Eightfold Path, this is the final Commandment. In both cases, the climactic instruction fulfills all the others. The first nine Commandments prescribe patterns of behavior that help a society live in harmony. But from a behavioral perspective, this Commandment is superfluous. As long as we don't steal them, what does it matter if we covet the goods of others?

It matters because we are forfeiting our inner personal harmony, which is the root of social harmony. As long as we're caught up in making fantasy appointments with our neighbor's spouse, status, or possessions, we're sowing frustration and cultivating the temptation to try to relieve it through stealing, lying, adultery, and all the rest. Then, if we yield to those temptations, we'll reap disappointment anyway, as the habit of coveting propels us into desiring the *next* forbidden fruit.

One night the Zen hermit-poet Ryokan comes home to his tiny hut to find that a thief has taken his few possessions. (In one version of the story, he catches the thief in the act and, sorry there's so little to steal, gives him the clothes off his back.) Afterward he sits down and writes:

> *The thief left it there*
> *There in the window frame—*
> *The shining moon.*

The thief is to be pitied because, no matter how many goods he accumulates, he'll always be poor, caught up in coveting the next thing and the next. But Ryokan is rich beyond measure. Not hypnotized by his own grasping, he has the clear vision to see the completely satisfying inherent beauty of existence itself, represented here by the moon.

Each of us is the thief, coveting this and that and mentally investing it with the power to fulfill us—an investment that must sooner or later go bust. But each of us is also Ryokan, with the ability to fully enjoy the moment, with material toys or without them. We keep choosing which one to be. To covet is to cultivate the delusion that a satisfactory life requires something we don't have—to blind ourselves to our own natural satori, our perception of the self-sufficient splendor of life as is.

> *It will not be said, "Look, here it is," or "Look, there it is." Rather, the father's kingdom is spread out upon the earth, and people do not see it.*
>
> —THE GOSPEL OF THOMAS

That is, the heaven we seek is fully present in whatever is at hand, without exception. So every time you covet better goods or higher status or, for that matter, more enlightened consciousness, you're looking right past that which is far more glorious than anything you could ever think of coveting. Every time I get lost in wishing I were in Bermuda or on Lake Como, or in some heavenly realm or nirvanic state, it's as if the kingdom of heaven, in whatever overlooked form is at hand, responds, "So what am I—chopped liver?"

SWEET NOTHINGS

It's important, then, that spiritual practice not just become a new, exotic form of expectation. We're chanting to chant, not to get anywhere or accomplish anything. We're acting with kindness to act with kindness, not to fulfill our duty or earn brownie points for the hereafter. We're praying to pray, not for any reward or response. (We're saying nothing for no reason; when you're in love, you whisper sweet nothings in your beloved's ear.) And we're sitting ("meditating") to sit, not to achieve some kind of cosmic consciousness.

True, there's a paradox here—one of the central paradoxes of spiritual practice. On the one hand, there *is* a goal. The great teachers entice us with glowing descriptions of nirvana or the kingdom of heaven; without some sense of a payoff we wouldn't take valuable time to engage in these practices. Yet these same teachers say that the *way* to the goal is to abide in goallessness—and that, having attained it, one sees that the division of "path" and "goal" was artificial all along. "How wonderful, how wonderful! All things are enlightened just as they are!" exclaimed the Buddha. But he said that only *after* he

attained enlightenment. In this business, if you don't run into paradox you haven't run far enough.

I once saw Charles throw an entire retreat into uproar by declar-
ing that meditation is completely useless. Of course, its uselessness
is exactly the reason for practicing it, to get off the hamster wheel of
pursuing our many useful appointments.

> *All men know the utility of useful things. Few men
> know the utility of futility.*
>
> —CHUANG-TZU

But meditation loses its useful uselessness if we turn it into an appointment with nirvana. Just do it. No, not even that.

> *You do not need to leave your room. Remain sitting at
> your table and listen. Do not even listen, simply wait.
> Do not even wait, be quite still and solitary. The world
> will freely offer itself to you to be unmasked, it has no
> choice, it will roll in ecstasy at your feet.*
>
> —KAFKA

Chögyam Trungpa Rinpoche said, "Enlightenment is the ego's
ultimate disappointment." That's because ego—the grasping, expecting aspect of mind—makes enlightenment the ultimate appointment. There's nothing unsatisfactory about enlightenment; it's
ego that doesn't measure up, just as a six-year-old might be disappointed in his first opera. The good news is that *this* disappointment
is the final stripping away of our ability to get caught up in appointments. This opera makes the kid grow up.

Then we stop spending our lives making appointments for some Godot or other to appear and fix what's not broken. After untold fruitless days of waiting for Godot (who, like free beer, is always coming tomorrow), Vladimir the tramp declares:

> *We have kept our appointment and that's an end to that.*
> *We are not saints, but we have kept our appointment.*
> *How many people can boast as much?*

His companion Estragon replies, "Billions."

But *you're* free. In any instant, this instant, you can make it billions minus one.

8.

BLESS
EVERYONE

*The saints are what they are, not because their
sanctity makes them admirable to others, but because the gift of sainthood makes it possible for
them to admire everybody else.*

—THOMAS MERTON

Boy, everyone is stupid except me!

—HOMER SIMPSON
(MOMENTS BEFORE
ACCIDENTALLY SETTING
HIS HOUSE ON FIRE)

The *Gilligan's Island* theory of alienation goes something like this:
When we confidently set sail on our voyage of life, it looks easy at
first—just a three-hour tour. But at some point the weather starts
getting rough and our tiny ship is tossed. We wind up feeling
stranded on an uncharted desert isle. So, to cure our isolation, we

try every attitude and resource we can—good-natured bumbling (Gilligan), domineering bluster (the Skipper), money and status (the Millionaire and His Wife), sex and fame (the Movie Star), intellect and its inventions, including ingenious electronic communication devices (the Professor), and timid naïveté (Mary Ann). But somehow, in episode after episode, we're still marooned.

A solution we may have learned in temple, church, or mosque is to love everyone, and that's a brilliant, inspiring, absolutely correct answer. But if we could do that, we wouldn't be stranded on this island in the first place. Fortunately, there's something easier than loving—blessing—and it primes the pump for love. Just as you are, you can extend your blessing to everyone, just as they are. Blessing is a come-as-you-are party.

There's nothing mystical about blessing people. In its most basic sense, it means to wish them well, to consciously will them happiness and freedom from suffering. For that matter, even love is not some special, exalted mood that we need to manufacture, or something that's difficult or embarrassing. It's not an attitude we can construct but the sparkling-clear perception that remains when attitudes get out of the way. As we gradually drop our concepts and see people as they are, love is the spontaneous appreciation that's left.

Why do fools fall in love?
—FRANKIE LYMON AND THE TEENAGERS

Why? Because love, like foolishness, is a state free of thought. Stepping up to love is like stepping up to the plate, and, as Yogi Berra asked, "How can you hit and think at the same time?"

Love to faults is always blind,
Always is to joy inclin'd,
Lawless, wing'd, and unconfin'd,
And breaks all chains from every mind.

—WILLIAM BLAKE

So if we really want to break the chains from our mind, the prescription is clear: look past what our mind thinks about people and love them all, whether good guys or bad. But because this is much too daunting an assignment for most mortals, we can start by blessing them.

BAD GUYS

In the process, we may make a startling discovery. There *are* no bad guys: that's only in cheesy movies. That's why our greatest artists—Chaucer, Shakespeare, Rembrandt, Hitchcock—can't portray a villain without showing that he is also a tender, vulnerable, even lovable human, groping in the dark for happiness and tripping again and again on his own limitations . . . kind of like us. For the schlock filmmaker or novelist, creating two-dimensional villains is easy, but we don't want to live schlock lives. Shakespeare's Claudius or Raymond Burr as the murderer in *Rear Window* move us to respond from a deeper level of our being than the thinking mind that knows their flaws; they short-circuit our logic boards and make us respond from the heart.

Of course, bad guys do bad things, and *that* we can't condone. This is where it gets challenging—and interesting.

Buddha prohibited unwholesome actions, but did not tell
us to hate those who practice unwholesome actions.

—DOGEN

Can we work, say, to eliminate torture from the world while opening ourselves enough to bless the torturers along with their victims?
If we can, our thoughts and actions will be very powerful. Nelson
Mandela spent a quarter of a century imprisoned under the most
brutal conditions, but refused to give in to hatred for his oppressors.
"At some point," he said, "I realized it was not productive." The result was that he won over his guards and eventually the conscience of
the world.

Here also we can find the deeper value of the Commandment,
"Do not bear false witness against your neighbor." On the outer, behavioral level, it's enough to refrain from speaking untruths about
what our neighbor *does*, but if we're determined to get clear on the
level of inner awareness, we must also leave off thinking and feeling
untruths about what he *is*. The guy who smashes his empty beer bottle on my sidewalk has *done* something heinous. But as I sweep up the
pieces I'm bearing false witness if I mutter that he *is* a bum (or
blighter, bounder, budmash, cad, creep, cur, and so on through the
thesaurus). He *is* pure, radiant existence, just like me. And the more
room I give him to be that, the more room I find—mysteriously,
miraculously—for *me* to be that.

Do not judge, so that you may not be judged. For with
the judgment you make you will be judged, and the mea-
sure you give will be the measure you get.

—MATTHEW 7:1–2

132

And if you don't underestimate me,
I won't underestimate you.

—BOB DYLAN

BEGGARS AND BANQUETS

To begin the process of blessing, then, there are a few things we can do, or, rather, leave off doing. One thing to renounce is *resentment*—that almost irresistibly delicious bitterness over the success and happiness of others. (For me it comes with seeing other writers' books—far less worthy than mine, of course—crowd the store windows and best-seller lists.) Many people have a habit, when a friend tells them news of some good fortune, of exclaiming, "I hate you!" This is supposed to be a joke, but it's not a very good one.

There's a Tibetan tale about a jealous beggar who passes his days just outside the palace wall, muttering, "Why does *he* get to be the king and enjoy all those luxuries? Someone should cut his head off and make *me* king!" One day, exhausted by rage, the beggar falls asleep on the ground, and as the king's chariot passes through the gate it rolls over him and cuts off *his* head. Without necessarily believing in such literal karmic retribution, we can see the tale's psychological accuracy: our resentment of others fails to transfer even a shred of their happiness to us, but succeeds in choking our minds with negativity.

So, stop . . . if you want to be free.

The second renunciation, the mirror twin of the first, is *schadenfreude*: pleasure derived from the misery of others. (Think of bratty Nelson on *The Simpsons*, with his triumphant "*Ha*-ha!") This is popular stuff. If the total energy of all the schadenfreude produced on this planet every day could somehow be harnessed, it could probably power all our heavy industry. When our scheming rival finally gets his comeuppance, when some self-righteous politician or phony holy man flames out in scandal, it's one thing to cheer for the triumph of justice and decency; it's quite another to smack our lips in a tasty "Gotcha!" The joy we drink from the suffering of a fellow being is polluted at the source. There's a purer, more expansive joy in turning that cup down.

So, stop . . . if you want to be free. Tie yourself to the mast. Don't *suppress* either resentment or schadenfreude, but whenever one of them arises, acknowledge again that it merely poisons your own heart while doing nothing to its intended target. Then let it go. This is a venture into uncharted territory and may be difficult. With practice it gets easier. But if it's too hard at first, start by just *noticing* how many such negative thoughts you have. Put a little piece of paper in your pocket and keep a tally through the day. You may be shocked. After a few days of making this unconscious habit conscious, you'll probably find the mind spontaneously turning away from these thoughts as they come up.

There are also more subtle forms of antiblessing to renounce. Most of us, for example, maintain an unwritten list of those who, we feel, have withheld or withdrawn love from us. Whether they're ex-paramours or problematic parents, just the thought of them triggers defensive hostility. These are exactly the people we should make a special point of blessing. If we recognize and undercut that hostile reflex rather than be carried away by it, it presents a wonderful opportunity to liberate ourselves.

Then there's our unwritten list of losers, those who (we've

decided) are not as cool or smart or attractive as we are, or not as moral or enlightened. Merely hearing their names, we may smirk with irony, snort with contempt. It's tempting to just dismiss them—"Oh, that poseur," "That nut case," "That ridiculous fashion casualty," "That ignorant bigot," "That contemptible thug"— but it's at a price. By closing our hearts to them, we cut off our own expansiveness. Jesus offers shrewd advice here:

> *When you make a feast, call the poor, the maimed, the lame, the blind.*

> —LUKE 14:13

Now *that's* a challenge. To my banquet of life I'm to invite the ones I've written off as clumsy losers—the ones who are too poor to pay my dues, too maimed to make my grade, too lame to walk my walk, too blind to see my way—the ones I'm sure will stink up the party. The decision to bless everyone is the decision never to write anyone off again, including (especially) life's alleged losers. Maybe we don't literally invite them to our table, maybe realistically we're going to skip *their* parties or vote them out of office, maybe in their blindness they've done things for which we must lock them in jail, but we can make the commitment to drop our scorn and stop locking them out of our heart.

EXORCISM

That commitment is difficult, but there are techniques, skillful means to make it easier. A useful first step is to recognize that our judgment of others is rooted in self-judgment. Sit down with a piece of paper and make a list of all the reasons why you think (perhaps secretly) that you're virtuous or cool—why you deserve a seat at the banquet. Then list all the reasons why you fear you're wretched or uncool. Be completely honest. Then throw the list away. The simple act of dragging these unacknowledged judgments into the light of day shows you, first of all, how trivial most of them are. Having relaxed your self-judgment, you'll find that your need to judge others starts to relax as well.

The really stubborn insecurities may require some more dramatic form of exorcism. I used to teach public speaking, an activity that ranks above death in most surveys of people's greatest fears. I found that the most effective way to loosen my students up was to begin a session with a Monty Python–style Silly Walks contest. They quickly started egging each other on, and soon they were vying to outdo each other: strutting, twitching, flapping, bobbing, wiggling, whooping, barking. Once they had made complete fools of themselves in front of each other—and didn't die or get pregnant—they found it much easier to speak before a group without worrying about making fools of themselves.

FROM THE HEART

If you were raised in a religion, you probably learned hymns of blessing that you can still sing or benedictions that you can still recite. A lovely one is, "May the peace of God, which passeth all understanding, be with you now and forever." These are very powerful when you let yourself really hear the words, take them to heart, and consciously direct them toward specific people. You can start with those you like and then, as you warm up, work your way to those whose guts you hate. If you don't feel a genuine connection with any traditional blessing formulas, make up your own. You can also revisit the simple bedtime prayer you may have said as a child: "God bless Mommy, God bless Daddy . . ." Just don't stop with Grandma and Grandpa—keep going.

There are also wordless methods of blessing. Tibetan practice includes one called *tonglen*. This is a hardcore technique, recommended for serious practitioners who meditate regularly and are emotionally stable. Sit with eyes closed and allow another person's image to arise in the space before you (or if you find it easier, just feel his or her presence). Let the sense of separation between the two of you melt. Imagine all the person's suffering, confusion, and worry, surrounding him or her as a cloud of dark, hot, toxic smoke. Then, as you inhale, draw the smoke into your heart and purify it, transforming it into pure white light. As you exhale, breathe out happiness and healing in the form of that light, and shower the other person with it.

Later you can do tonglen for yourself, for situations, families, groups, nations, and eventually all the beings in the universe. You can do it with eyes open as you stand in line or walk down the street. But don't expand the scope of the exercise so quickly that it becomes merely conceptual; this should be something you *feel*. And don't use it as a cosmic cop-out, a spiritual form of "I gave at the office." When you see misery footage on the evening news, you can do tonglen for the flood victims, but don't forget to send a check.

This is the experience of my friend Lowell:

I was at the hospital, visiting a friend who was seriously ill. As usual in that setting, I felt uneasy, not wanting to be there, emotionally trying to push the whole situation away. So when my friend dozed off I did tonglen for her, breathing in her illness and fear and breathing out health and ease.

At some point I realized I should include my own fear in what I was transforming, so I did that. But then that also started to feel limited, so I included all the other patients in the hospital. Then I had the thought that the doctors and the staff were as mortal and scared as anyone else— their uniforms and professional attitudes couldn't protect them—so I included them too.

Afterward I felt much more at ease. When my friend woke up, the visit felt less strained, more intimate. My invisible shield was gone. And somehow she seemed to pick up on that and was more at ease as well.

Yes, mentally sucking in someone else's disease is scary, but blasting through the fear that isolates us is exactly the point. If you want to expand your heart, tonglen is the goods. You really can love anyone some of the time, and you can inch toward loving everyone all the time. "I love you" turns out to be not just an abstract sentiment but a vivid experience, a radiance that streams from our heart center and showers upon others. Maybe this is why we identify love with the heart (rather than the liver or gallbladder). Valentine hearts probably have nothing to do with the fist-sized organ that pumps our blood but represent the heart *center*, that radiant energy nexus which is a subtle door between inner awareness-space and the outer world of other beings. We see it in the pictures of Jesus of the Sacred Heart, pulling his robe open at the chest to reveal beams of love-light blazing outward to cleanse the world. It's exciting to discover that, if we take him as a role model and not just an icon, we can do that ourselves.

The Gaelic phrase for "I love you" literally means "I'm melting for you." Tonglen helps melt the solid, opaque shell (what we call "self") between our inner space and the outer world. By reversing our habit of trying to keep all the pain, craziness, and other unpleasant stuff outside and all the pleasant stuff inside, tonglen breaks down the very notion of inside and outside, which is the basis of alienation. It conquers fear by opening to that which scares us most. Perfect love—the love in which melting is complete—casteth out all fear.

POURING SYRUP

You can also invent your own ways of blessing people. Every time you hear a siren you can remember that someone like you is in trouble and wish them the best. Here in New Jersey we have Waving Willie, a retired man who spends his days sitting in a lawn chair on the side of the highway, waving to the cars as they go by. A high-school teacher I know does what he calls "mug shot mojo," browsing through old yearbooks, gazing at the faces of former students, and sending them positive energy. My mailman Dave makes a habit of smiling and sharing a cheery greeting with everybody he meets on his route, doing his best to spread friendliness and happiness through his little piece of the world. Why not? You can make like Dave with everyone from your boss or employees to the people who pump your gas and bag your groceries.

There's a certain amount of time-space structure to your life that you can't do much about: maybe you work in an office cubicle and have to follow a schedule. That structure is sort of like the indentations in a waffle. But the kind of syrup you pour on the waffle—the interpersonal energy that sloshes around within the structure—is up to the people in it, and it only takes one person to start transforming it into something more loose and friendly and fun. Sometimes, in the course of the day, you may find yourself stuck in lame, tedious conversations. You don't care about what the other people are saying, but you can care about *them*. Rather than squirm with boredom, use this as an opportunity to silently shower them with lovingkindness. It's a dirty job, but someone's gotta do it.

THE TRUE FLOWERS

In Tibetan tradition, blessing is also spread by reciting the Mantra of Great Compassion, OM MANI PADME HŪNG (pronounced *om mah-nee pay-may hoong*). Volumes have been written about these six syllables, with their many layers of meaning and their resonance beyond meaning. On a literal level, the gist is, "The jewel [mani] is in the lotus [padme]." The jewel of life, the precious treasure of happiness which we all seek at every moment, is to be found wherever the lotus flower grows—and since the lotus grows in profusion, sometimes covering the surface of ponds and lakes, it is understood metaphorically to grow everywhere. So, because the jewel of supreme happiness is already at the heart of everyone and everything, blessedness does not have to be added but only acknowledged, enlivened within our perception. All things and people are already the perfect blossoms of perfect being.

> *People, yes people are the true flowers of life: and it has been a most precious pleasure to have temporarily strolled in your garden.*
>
> —LORD BUCKLEY

Blessing everyone, then, really means seeing that everyone is already blessed. This view saves us from the arrogance of supposing that we have some great spiritual power that we stoop to confer upon others. We don't share with them from the heights of our luminous awareness but notice that they are the luminosity.

Here's an exercise in enlightened people-watching:

Take a stroll through one of our great democratic spaces—a movie theater lobby, the food court at the local mall, the boardwalk in July. If you're like me, you'll find yourself automatically sizing people up, seeing (so you think) the limits of their vision. That lame-o suburban mom, that scary biker—*they* don't know the score. Of course, you're not seeing them at all, but judging them on the basis of the bodies and social roles in which they're dressed.

> *Dans les yeux les plus sombres s'enferment les plus claires.*
> *(In the darkest eyes are hidden the brightest eyes.)*
>
> —PAUL ELUARD

The reality is that you have no idea what waves of boundless love the mom feels for her kids, or what vistas of expansive silence the biker experiences when he's rolling down the highway. (And maybe the biker loves his kids deeply and the mom rides a Harley on weekends.) The juice of life is available to everyone all the time; we have no idea who's drinking it how.

The exercise, then, is simply to *notice* your mind making these judgments and, over and over again, let them go. If you like, you can supercharge the process by silently chanting the Mani mantra or any other formula that works for you. Wherever a constricted stereotype was, smash it open to reveal the space where anything is possible.

FROGS AND ANTS

So, in case you're wondering what to do while the service rep has you on hold, or you're packed into the crowded elevator, or you're coming home in the subway car full of weary commuters avoiding eye contact, you can mentally shower everyone with your favorite blessing prayer, or do tonglen for them, or (if you dare) just smile at them, or (if you can) just perceive them in the full blossoming of their natural glory. As we've seen, devotion means kissing the frog. Blessing means blowing kisses to the whole frog pond.

On the widest level, this process embraces all conscious beings. "Bless everyone" means bless not just every human but every little eddy in the great stream of life that perceives itself as separate: animals, birds, fish, insects, all beings seen and unseen. (Saint Francis, when he "preached" to the birds, was probably up to something like this.) Again, it's not that they need our blessing. As the corrective to our narrowed vision, the cure for our alienation, we need to bless them.

> *Once in camp I put a log on top of the fire and it was full of ants. As it commenced to burn, the ants swarmed out and . . . fell off into the fire. I remember thinking at the time that it was the end of the world and a splendid chance to be a messiah and lift the log off the fire and throw it out where the ants could get off onto the ground. But I did not do anything but throw a tin cup of water on the log, so that I would have the cup empty to put whiskey in before I added water to it. I think the cup of water on the burning log only steamed the ants.*
>
> —ERNEST HEMINGWAY, *A FAREWELL TO ARMS*

If we don't care about the ants, why should we expect God or the universe or existence to care about us? True, we can't save every ant from the fire. We can't buy every lamb out of bondage before it reaches the slaughterhouse, and we can't save every starving African child we see on TV. But we can help some of them and bless all of them, and so erode our separateness.

Of course, there's another paradox here. Because blessing others opens *our* heart, gives *us* a good feeling, makes *us* good Christians (or Muslims or Hindus or whatever we are), this outpouring of self-lessness is actually selfish.

> *I know myself, and I know the depth of my selfishness. I cannot be at ease (and to be at ease is my chief wish) if someone else is in pain, visibly or audibly or tactu-*

ally. Sometimes this is mistaken by the innocent for un-
selfishness. . . .

—GRAHAM GREENE, *THE QUIET AMERICAN*

Theologians have struggled with this paradox for centuries, but Shantideva resolved it 1300 years ago, explaining simply that we must start where we are. At first our altruism, like everything else, is tainted by selfishness—but it's a valid way (the only way) to set upon the path that eventually leads to pure, unselfish altruism.

Starting where we are also implies that to bless everyone we don't first have to purge all our old grudges and hatreds or untangle all our old feelings. That would be backwards; then no one could ever start. The process of blessing facilitates the untangling. You don't have to figure anything out, you don't have to be some other kind of person. Just choose to start.

In this age troubled by war, famine, disease, disasters,
and physical and mental suffering of all kinds, to think
even for an instant of the welfare of others is of incon-
ceivable merit.

—H. H. DILGO KHYENTSE RINPOCHE

Just take the first step of blessing others, and life changes in inconceivable ways.

9.

DISCONNECT
THE DOTS

"All right!" said the [Cheshire] Cat; and this
time it vanished quite slowly, beginning with the
end of the tail, and ending with the grin, which
remained some time after the rest of it had gone.

—LEWIS CARROLL, *ALICE'S*
ADVENTURES IN WONDERLAND

We see water, a few small sloops and rowboats, a grove, a park, three dogs, some two dozen people in bustles or top hats lounging or strolling, some with parasols, one with a pet monkey on a leash. But if we look closer we see that there's no water, no park, no people, no monkey . . . just a lot of pastel dots. In fact we're looking at Seurat's pointillist masterpiece, *A Sunday Afternoon on the Island of La Grande Jatte.* The way this painting emerges from dots provides a valuable clue to our understanding of what's what, who we are, and, most important, how we can be free.

What if there are really no "things" but only dots, pixels, bits of sensory data? What if "things" emerge from the connections we imagine between the dots?

Consider the Big Dipper. Does it exist? Well, yes and no. We see it, we learn about it in school, it might save our lives by helping us locate the North Star when we're lost in the woods. Yet "it" is a group of stars millions of light years apart, with no astronomical relationship except that, as viewed from our vantage point on Earth, they accidentally appear to be neighbors. The connecting lines are drawn only in our minds, yet it's hard to look up at those stars and *not* see the Dipper.

That's all right, but if we start to think that the Dipper is "real," things get tricky. One problem is that some people look at the same stars and see Ursa Major, the Great Bear; others see the Plough. All our philosophies might be different ways to connect the unconnected dots of raw experience; people have fought wars and gone to the stake over which lines are "right." We like to connect dots into perfect patterns that make perfect sense, but in fact they're perfectly patternless, scattered in perfect open space.

Do not seek Truth, but merely cease to cherish opinion.

— S E N G - T S ' A N

Opinions are patterns of connection between perceived dots. When the dots fail to fit our pattern, we may even try to add, erase, or move a few as needed. (My mind is made up—don't confuse me with the facts.) If we could just drop those contrived patterns, then patternless truth, unsought, would be obvious.

Believing is seeing. This backward process can be seen in grand ideologies (the church's rejection of Galileo's data because they didn't fit the geocentric picture) as well as in everyday life. When my daughter reached the age where kids draw pictures of their families, I noticed that she kept using a brown crayon for my hair. One day I asked, "Why does she use brown instead of yellow?" Much amused, my family had to march me to the mirror before I would be convinced that the blond hair of my childhood had long since turned brown. I had grown so used to the idea of being blond that I literally didn't see what was before my eyes.

Even the raw sensory data from which we assemble our picture is far from absolute. A dog's sense of smell is some 500 times more sensitive than ours. While we generally define things visually, by the molecules that are lined up in tight groupings to reflect light (what we call surfaces), the dog presumably defines things by the more diffuse molecules that waft through the air and enter its nose. If we could inhabit a dog's awareness for a moment, we would see—or smell—a world that is fluid, shifting, airborne. We humans have a vivid sense of color because our ancestors' survival depended on distinguishing ripe fruit from unripe; birds of prey live in a world that is monochromatic but where the motion of a field mouse can be spotted from hundreds of meters up. Someone who's colorblind sees only one color where the rest of us see red and green; but a bee sees white and ultraviolet where we see only white.

THINGS

Many philosophers have understood that our perception is subjective. Kant spoke of *das Ding an sich*, "the thing as such," as something unknowable that underlies our perception. But even that is saying too much. The *an sich* part, the notion of underlying suchness, makes sense. But because we assemble things by connecting dots, outside our subjectivity there ain't no such *Ding*.

> *[T]he Buddha himself said with his own lips: . . ."Habitual patterns and conditioning of our thought processes . . . define and label appearances . . . objectifying them, forming them accordingly. All things are created by our own minds."*
>
> —THE FLIGHT OF THE GARUDA

Is there such a "thing" as a bank? The way I spend my time and energy is largely determined by the fact that the bank holds a mortgage on my house, but where is that bank? In the impressively solid-looking pillars outside the local branch office? In the corporate headquarters in another city? In the flow of digital data between ATMs and a warehouse full of computers somewhere in the desert? In the mind of the bank president as he plays with his kids on the weekend?

Is there such a thing as a book? Is *One Hundred Years of Solitude* this object sitting on my table, made of paper, glue, and ink? Is it all the copies all over the world? Or is it the elaborate ballet of themes and images that once danced in the mind of Gabriel García Márquez and now dances sporadically in the minds of his readers? In that case, whenever no one on the planet is reading or remembering it, has it ceased to exist? Does it come back into existence when a new reader picks it up?

Is there such a thing as New York City? It shapes the lives of

millions of people, but what *is* it? The words printed in the munici-
pal charter? The ground underlying the streets and buildings? If so,
did it exist in the time of the Indians? If not, and if we could up-
root all the streets and buildings and transplant them to the moon,
would *that* be New York City? Maybe it's more like an essence, a flavor, something I can taste by watching a Woody Allen movie or
hearing Sinatra sing "New York, New York." But then if I watch the
movie or hear the song in Tokyo, is New York in Tokyo?

As I look out my window, I see three piles of leaves sitting at the
curb. A breeze stirs the leaves. A few blow from one pile to another,
and a few blow into the street. Am I still looking at those three piles?
Well, sure, we might say, the pile has an identity that's independent
of a few shifting leaves. Then suppose I go down to the curb, pick
up one leaf from Pile A, and add it to Pile B. Then another, then another, till Pile A is gone. If the pile exists independent of its leaves,
where is it now? Perhaps every "thing" is like a pile of leaves—just a
concatenation of components, linked in our minds and given a name.

Perhaps the leaf is the real "thing." But a leaf is also a concatenation of components. We can deconstruct the leaf to get stem,
veins, capillaries; then take any of those components and break it
down into cells; then break down the cell into mitochondrion, vac-
uole, chloroplast, and so forth; and keep on through molecules to
atoms, which are mostly empty space, enlivened by the rare presence
of a particle like an electron, which on closer examination can't quite
be pinned down as a particle because it's sort of just energy and
maybe even just a probability wave, a mathematical chance that it
might turn up in a given location at a given time.

So even our dots are barely dots.

Then, if all these things are not things after all, perhaps it's fairer to call them processes, or events. But an event is also a con-catenation of components (smaller events, which are in turn made of yet smaller events), subjectively selected and connected. This ap-plies whether we're writing and rewriting world history or our per-sonal history. Stuff happens; then we connect the dots with story lines that support the themes we've imagined and the characters as we've cast them. The dots that don't fit our story line, we leave out. Thus we create drama and, if we're especially creative, neurosis. (It's our party and we'll cry if we want to.) Certainly to function in the world we need to perceive and respond to events and patterns, just as we need to rake our leaves. But just as with the leaves, the closer we look at those events, the emptier they are, and the more our drama and trauma are defused.

> *There must be some way to undone what you done done.*
>
> —ALGONQUIN J. CALHOUN

US

Is there *anything* solid and definable in the midst of all this empti-ness? At least there's *us* . . . isn't there?

Let's see. By "us" do we mean the body? If so, you'd better stop trimming your toenails, because you're throwing "you" away. And if you don't reside in your toenail, where do you reside? Liver? Pan-creas? Head? Many people point to their head when they say "me," and have a strong subjective sense of dwelling somewhere inside it. But is that just because the organs of our most dominant senses happen to converge in a sort of perspectival vanishing point in the middle of the skull? What if our eyes were mounted on our elbows and our ears on our knees? Where would "we" be then?

If we're not in any one part, maybe we're somehow the body as a whole. But does the body have any more permanent cohesiveness than a pile of leaves? Stuff is being added and eliminated all the time. As long as we can keep a sufficient number of components functioning in a sufficiently coordinated relationship, people will continue to point at the whole shebang and say, "There's Dean." But they're still just components. Some Tibetan ritual practices use drums made from human skulls and trumpets made from human thigh bones. Playing them reminds practitioners that their own bones are mere connect-the-dots, that the-head-bone-connected-to-the-neck-bone and the-thigh-bone-connected-to-the-knee-bone for a limited time only. Eventually they'll be disconnected beyond our control, ready or not. If we mentally practice disconnecting them now, it's not so astonishing when it happens later.

Surely, though, we must be something more than, or other than, the sum of our parts. There must be a ghost in the machine, some kind of "self." Descartes famously declared that the very act of doubting our existence proved the existence of the doubter: "I think, therefore I am." But does the thinking of thoughts really imply a separate entity, a "thinker," any more than the blowing of the wind implies a separate "blower"? The wind *is* the blowing. (When there's a *lot* of blowing we even give it a name, like the ones we give ourselves; we call it Hurricane Floyd, but where does Floyd retire to when the blowing stops?) Hasn't Descartes stacked the deck anyway by starting his sentence with "I"? All we can really say is, "Thinking is taking place, therefore thinking is taking place."

He would answer to "Hi!" or to any loud cry
Such as "Fry me!" or "Fritter my wig!"
To "What-you-may-call-um!" or "What-was-his-name!"
But especially "Thing-um-a-jig!"

—LEWIS CARROLL

Maybe, then, the "self" is just a kind of thing-um-a-jig, a response we conjure up in answer to the "loud cries" of mental and sensory experiences, a connecting pattern we draw between the dots of thoughts.

But don't take my word for it. Keep looking. You can't conclude that there's no self till you've exhausted all the places where one might be hiding. It's like a big game of "Where's Waldo?," one so huge it covers the entirety of our experience. We have to search every inch of the picture till we've found him. If we can't, then we can conclude that Waldo's gone AWOL.

FIND THE MIND

What about the soul, or the mind?

"Soul" we can't say much about. That's a theological term, part of a belief system, and thus not subject to the kind of straightforward experiential method we're attempting here. "Mind" we should be able to approach experientially, since we experience everything else *through* the mind; but can we experience the mind itself?

Please glance around the room and notice whatever colors are present. Then notice the color of your mind. That is, what color is the awareness *within which* the colors of the room are experienced? (Check it out—be a good scientist!) You probably notice that awareness is *no* color, but rather a colorlessness that admits all colors, like a clear window. Then what *shape* is your mind? Again, it allows us to perceive all shapes, but has none of its own. After a little more investigation, we can probably agree that mind also has no size, sound, smell, flavor, texture, temperature, gender, or any other limited quality.

Neither is it a limited mental state. Think of a pleasant scene from your past, something that makes you feel happiness. Then think of a scene that makes you feel sadness. By observing carefully, you'll find that the feelings of happy and sad, just like colors or sounds, are experienced *within* mind, but mind itself remains flavorless, spacious, free. We can never *be* happy or sad, but always *are* the perfect, colorless open space within which happy and sad feelings come and go.

Then what's all this stuff I thought was uniquely, unalterably me—my opinions, my sense of humor, my remembered history? More empty dots floating in empty space. All of it just passing through, some rapidly, some lingering long enough for us to fixate on and identify with. But we're not the characteristics and we're not the container of the characteristics. There *is* no container.

I ain't a Kat . . . and I ain't Krazy.

—KRAZY KAT

This is why people under the influence of psychedelics sometimes think that everything is "melting." They're actually catching a glimpse of the fact that it never solidly existed to begin with. Likewise, when they think they're "dying," they're glimpsing the fact that *they* never solidly existed either.

We're not the constellations. We're not the stars. If we're anything, we're the endless sky within which the stars appear to appear.
Finally there's nothing we can say.

> *"I can't explain myself, I'm afraid, sir," said Alice,*
> *"because I'm not myself, you see."*
> *"I don't see," said the Caterpillar.*
>
> —LEWIS CARROLL, *ALICE'S*
> *ADVENTURES IN WONDERLAND*

But while we can't explain it, we can live it, through simple, open
awareness. This is freedom. We still feel happiness and sadness, we
still think Republican or Democratic thoughts, but, no longer identified with our feelings and thoughts, we're free from *being* sad or
happy, Republicans or Democrats. We are likewise free from suffering—not that pain is absent, but that we are free even in its presence, perceiving it as yet another color painted upon the surface of
the mind's unfathomable colorlessness.

Perhaps you've had the experience of trying to fulfill some standard or image—to be a certain kind of cool or sexy or wise or non-
chalant, or a good follower of some ideology. Then, eventually, you
gave it up. After the initial disorientation, you probably felt pro-
foundly liberated. As Coco Chanel once said, "How many cares one
loses when one decides not to be something but to be someone."
How many *more* cares one loses when one decides not even to be
someone but just to *be*. It takes a lot of surface tension to hold all
those dots in place, to keep them consistent with whoever we've decided we are. No pretension, no tension.

In fact, we so crave this freedom that if we don't know how to disconnect our own dots internally through awareness practice we intuitively seek some external method, even if it's temporary: drugs, booze, headbanging music, and movies with bigger and louder explosions are some popular favorites. Or we may find sneaky ways to destroy ourselves, like Oedipus or Lear, Willy Loman or Richard Nixon, each one the agent of his own destruction, or deconstruction. The king must fall so that he may discover his true self, which is non-king and non-self.

As long as we think we're a self, we're trapped in the drama of "good" and "bad" things happening to it. We're like characters in a movie who suffer disasters and enjoy triumphs. But if we're no longer stuck looking through a single character's eyes, no matter what happens to that character we can enjoy the movie.

CLOSE ENCOUNTERS

Shit happens. That's a rough translation of the Buddha's First Noble Truth. We can't make that go away; but, says the Third Noble Truth, we can make *us* go away, or, more accurately, we can find that we were never here and that there's therefore no one for the shit to stick to. Lots still happens, but it's all vacant lots. Since we're essentially empty openness and everything else is essentially empty openness, even our closest encounters with the most solid apparent reality (fist hits jaw, car hits tree, nail pierces hand) are openness interacting openly with openness. Every interaction becomes like two galaxies passing through one another—each contains billions of stars, but because they're mostly empty space, no two stars collide.

Of course if a nail goes through my hand, I'll feel it and I'll cry.

Even though it's empty, it all continues to function, and that includes both events and our emotional responses to them. People often fear that enlightenment means you're left without your emotions, like the folks in *Invasion of the Body Snatchers* whose personalities have been sucked up by alien peapods. But it's just the opposite: your emotions are left without "you." In fact, it's us unenlightened folk who keep trying to suppress our emotions, because the illusory "I" that we cherish is so fragile and our emotions are so powerful.

Actually, the pertinent movie moment here is Fred Astaire and Ginger Rogers dancing "Cheek to Cheek" in *Top Hat*—she in that fabulous dress of white satin and marabou feathers, he the most elegant man ever to wear a tux. They execute the same movements as ordinary humans do—lifting their feet, bending their elbows, turning their heads—but somehow they have been purged of selfhood, the heavy substantiality that keeps humans earthbound.

> *The enlightened art of the bodhisattva is to appear to move in the transparent sphere of conventional characteristics and harmoniously functioning causality, while remaining totally awake to . . . sheer Reality.*
>
> —PRAJNAPARAMITA SUTRA

Fred and Ginger dance their way through a ritualized sequence of human activities and emotions—courtship, dejection, elation—but all on a plane of miraculous lightness, our childhood dreams of levitation made visible. Appropriately, Fred sings, "Heaven—I'm in heaven!" The sublime grace with which they move is an inkling of that grace which is the kingdom of heaven.

Personal relationships, as they move to this level, become, like Fred and Ginger, lighter than air. Yet our dancing continues. "I love you" becomes an increasingly interesting proposition as the constructs of "I" and "you" gradually evaporate. All the heavy idealized or demonized versions of the "you" that I was projecting and the "I" that was projecting them—delightfully, refreshingly gone. What's left? Whatever I am loves whatever you are: two ever-deepening mysteries pouring into one another. With no constricted selves to separate us, dancing cheek to cheek is like being interpenetrating galaxies.

Once my wife wrote me a valentine:

> *Roses are empty,*
> *Violets are empty,*
> *Sugar is empty,*
> *And so are you.*

She was alluding to the Buddhist term *shunyata*, which is correctly translated as "emptiness" but frequently misunderstood. It doesn't mean a gaping void, a grim vacuum, a black hole, an arid existential desert. It means empty of boundaries, empty of definability, empty of selfhood and therefore of separateness.

> *This vastness is not empty or a void or impersonal*
> *but filled with the incandescent nectar of selfless love,*
> *tender joy, and gratitude.*
>
> —PRAJNAPARAMITA SUTRA

JUMP IN

The Heart Sutra says:

> *Form is no other than emptiness, emptiness no other than form.*
> *Form is exactly emptiness, emptiness exactly form.*

This is a wildly fantastic proposition, that the entire universe of structures is, upon closer examination, wide-open structurelessness; that all that somethin' is just nothin' in drag. But this is consistent with our discovery that things break down into dots, dots break down into space, and space opens out into unconstricted, undefinable empty awareness.

We seek the fundamental truth of existence. "Fundament" means bottom: we want to know what the truth is at bottom, the very ground floor of reality. But if there were a ground floor, there would have to be some kind of ground or basement for it to rest on; so *that* would have to be the fundamental truth. But then *that* . . . So truth is bottomless. It just opens out and out and out, perpetual openingness. This means that our descriptions may be very clever, but they're just descriptions; that our most passionately held notions are notions only; that whatever we think, whatever we believe, the situation is bigger and barer than that.

If we insist on subscribing to any allegedly fundamental truth, or even to the idea that some unspecified something somewhere *must* be the fundamental truth, then, it could be said, we're fundamentalists. The alternative is to just stop clawing for truth, for the bottom, and rest in that bottomlessness. Just fall, like Alice, down the rabbit hole. And don't worry about falling *down*; it's also topless, sideless, and centerless. Fear not. Centuries of saints and bodhisattvas who've gone before have shouted loud and clear: Jump right in, the water's fine.

The imaginary lines with which we connect the dots are the bars of our imaginary prison. When we let them fall away, what remains is freedom. To disconnect the dots there's nothing we have to do, since they were never connected. We can keep playing "Where's Waldo?" and "Find the Mind" till we're convinced, and loosening our grip on storylines and opinions. Beyond that the method is simple, pure perception: nonjudgmental, unelaborated experience of the dots of actual experience in this moment . . . and this moment . . . and this moment . . .

10.

BE A MENSCH
AND ENJOY
THE JOKE

*I just like people with some Looney Tune in their
souls.*

—LESTER BANGS

But to live outside the law you must be honest.

—BOB DYLAN

Among the papers on my desk is one of my favorite photographs,
clipped a few years ago from a newspaper. It was taken at a convo-
cation of seven winners of the Nobel Peace Prize, who had gathered
to confer on strategies to end war throughout the world. Seated in a
chair is Archbishop Desmond Tutu of South Africa, the great cham-
pion of human rights. Standing behind him is His Holiness the
XIV Dalai Lama. Both are laughing uproariously. Bishop Tutu is
clutching his hat as the Dalai Lama, that old prankster, tries to
snatch it off.

For me, this photo captures exactly the way to be in the world. Serve humanity, attend to the most solemn of responsibilities, and then stand back and laugh. Work like a grown-up, play like a child. Be a mensch and enjoy the joke.

> *Be fully attentive to what you are doing, without ever taking subject, object, or action as having any true existence.*
>
> —H. H. DILGO KHYENTSE RINPOCHE

There's no adequate English equivalent for the Yiddish word "mensch." Stout fellow? Solid citizen? Conscientious individual? (Antonym: flake.) It literally means "man," in the sense of being truly human—what Africans call *ubuntu* or *botho*—not in a sense that has anything to do with gender.

> *The world is full of guys. Be a man. Don't be a guy.*
>
> —SAY ANYTHING

It's someone you can depend on, someone who takes care of business, who makes sure she's part of the solution instead of part of the problem, who is (as I heard one lama describe an especially effective assistant) high yield, low maintenance. It's what the early Buddhists called the Arya, the Noble Ones, noble not by birth or station but by superior inner qualities outwardly manifested. It's what Rocky knew he would be if he was still standing when the bell rang at the end of the fifteenth round: not just another bum from the neighborhood.

A mensch honors his commitments, keeps his word. A mensch

is a professional, doesn't slack off on the job. The great blues singer Joe Williams once found himself in a Maryland nightclub performing for all of three couples—everyone else in town was watching Muhammad Ali in a title fight. But Williams sang his heart out and, when later asked why, replied that as a child he had learned to do everything like it's the last thing you'll ever do. When a mensch thinks he's finished a job (cleaning up the kitchen, proofreading the report), he takes one more look to see what he's missed. Then he *really* finishes the job.

For that matter, mensches make a habit of looking around to see what needs doing in the first place. My old dentist, Dr. Brown, used to say, "See me now or see me later"—"now" meant a filling and "later" meant a root canal. A mensch deals with the problem now, whether it's fixing the leaky faucet or addressing his own neuroses. The child (of any age) puts it off till later, in the vain hope that later will never come.

Yet mensches don't make unreasonable demands on anyone, including themselves. They know they're human. They don't necessarily get rid of all their little foibles, but they acknowledge them and devise strategies to compensate for them. (A friend of mine tried to be on time for years and was always fifteen minutes late. He finally figured out that if he tried to be fifteen minutes early he could be on time.) Rather than fixate on their weaknesses, mensches take the attitude I once saw written on a T-shirt: I MAY NOT BE PERFECT, BUT PARTS OF ME ARE EXCELLENT.

A boss of mine once said, "There are two kinds of people in my organization: those who bring me results and those who bring me stories." H. L. Mencken said: "There are two kinds of people in the world: those who pay their bills and those who don't." We all know the second kind of person. They trail excuses and complications be-hind them like tin cans tied to a rear bumper. And we know the first type, even if they're rarer. A mensch brings results, pays her bills, and so does not further burden the world with tiresome excuses and avoidable chaos.

Movies have tried again and again to capture the essence of the mensch as he goes about his business with quiet, modest integrity, while less noble characters are caught up in fear, greed, and petty egotism. The classic example is Gary Cooper in *High Noon*. As Will Kane, the retiring sheriff, he has no obligation to protect his small town from the gang of killers who are due on the noon train. It doesn't matter that the town, which refuses to help him form a posse, doesn't deserve his help. It doesn't matter that he's as fright-ened as anyone else. (The anguished expression on Cooper's face is genuine: during filming he was suffering from a bleeding ulcer.) The famous shot of Kane, all alone on the dusty main street as he real-izes that this is how he must meet the killers, shows the spot where every mensch sooner or later must make his stand, taking responsi-bility for some thankless job with a dubious outcome. And after Kane survives the battle, the shot of him tossing his tin star into the dust signifies the mensch's renunciation of glory. He just does what needs to be done.

SPIDERS AND BUGS

Mensches don't take things for granted; they have the good manners to say, "Thank you." If you've eaten, there are a lot of people you can thank, starting with the cook. If you have a warm place to sleep, give thanks for that. If your life is pretty comfortable, you're luckier than most. It's good to give thanks for your luck and to know that all luck is temporary. Life, says a Yiddish proverb, is the greatest bargain; we get it for nothing. You're a guest in this world, and it would be impolite not to thank your hosts, or Host. We're made out of dumb matter—mud. Whatever comes our way, the fact that we get to experience anything at all is an incomprehensible miracle.

> *And I was some of the mud that got to sit up and look around. Lucky me, lucky mud.*
>
> —KURT VONNEGUT, *CAT'S CRADLE*

Mensches don't save their energy for some grand, melodramatic gesture to be made someday by the saint they plan to become. Rather, they live now in the thousand small, considerate acts that keep the world running: they hold onto their candy wrapper till they find a trash can, they put fresh toilet paper on the roll, they signal their turns (and dim their high beams and don't block the passing lane, thank you very much).

> *Student: Master, please teach me the first principle of Zen.*
> *Master: Have you had your meal?*
> *Student: Yes, sir.*
> *Master: Then you'd better wash your bowl.*

A mensch doesn't spend his life whining and blaming his problems on others. There's a story about a monk who feels distracted by a spider that dangles in front of his face every time he sits to meditate. He asks his teacher for a knife and permission to kill the spider. "Fine," says the teacher, "but first take this piece of chalk, and the next time the spider appears, mark an X on its belly." The next day, when the monk reports that he has done as instructed, the teacher tells him to lift his shirt. There, on his belly, is a large X. "Good thing I didn't give you that knife," says the teacher.

The point (I think) is that we like to suppose the source of our discontent lies outside ourselves. If I could just get rid of my noisy neighbor, or my pushy boss, or the Arabs or the Jews, or the Hutus or the Tutsis, *then* everything would be OK. But it never works because, implausible as it may sound, the annoyance we have ascribed to others actually comes from ourselves: X marks the spot. By compassionating with the perceived source of irritation instead of trying to wipe it out, we escape from the illusion that we can—or need to—eliminate anything.

This brings us to the Commandment, "You shall not murder." Most people know the older, more absolute, less accurate translation, "Thou shalt not kill," but, since murder means *unwarranted* killing, we're stuck with the weighty responsibility of deciding what's warranted. In the summer I can barely walk across my lawn without squishing some bugs, but when a bug wanders into my house I can take the time to relocate it with a piece of paper and a Dixie cup. I'll do whatever's necessary to defend my family from thugs, but that's different from rooting for thugs to be executed. And there are other things we might be murdering besides people's bodies: their confidence, their dignity, their trust. A mensch, at the very least, tries not to be a murderer.

If all this sounds hard, it is—if mensches weren't exceptional, there wouldn't be a special word for them. But it becomes easier as open awareness comes to pervade our lives. Before, we might have neglected replacing the toilet paper roll as we rushed off to do something more fun. As we grow in realization, we're less and less distracted by the prospect of some greater fulfillment than we're experiencing right now. It's *all* fun.

THE JOKE

And it's all funny. Being a mensch is made easier still by the second half of this Suggestion. Yes, there's much to be done, and the world really does depend, whether locally or globally, on our doing it. But all the while, there's a big running joke pervading the whole affair, and the joke's on us.

> *No human thing is of serious importance.*
>
> —PLATO

> *Don't take life so serious, son . . . it ain't nohow permanent.*
>
> —POGO

We're all temps around here. The entire drama of our life and our world, everything that seems so crucially important, is like a dream that eventually evaporates, along with the dreamer. If there's nothing after this world, then we vanish into such utter oblivion that it's as if it all never happened. If there is a next world or a next life, then what seemed like the whole story is part of a much bigger picture. Either way, our worries were blown out of proportion.

Another aspect of the joke—another reason to take things lightly—is that we actually have no idea what's going on. Imagine a plot of ground surrounded by a high circular wall. Imagine that you were born within its confines and have never seen beyond it. All your understanding of life derives solely from your experiences inside the wall. But suppose the wall keeps expanding to enclose an ever-widening area. This means that all your descriptions and formulations of how things are are merely provisional and must be constantly revised to account for new experiences.

This, the British Empiricist philosopher David Hume observed some three centuries ago, is precisely humanity's situation. All we know is all we know, and with each moment we know more; therefore, we never *know*. We predict future particulars based on general "laws," but those laws are based on past particulars. We can confidently state that mammals never lay eggs till we see our first platypus. So, because there's always more to be revealed, anything's possible—we could turn out to be mistaken about everything. Once the terror wore off, that might be exciting.

> *Conclusions are ignorance arrested on the path to less ignorance.*
>
> —LAO-TZU

We must, therefore, constantly reinvent our lives. Or rather we must recognize that, like it or not, they're being reinvented for us, and that it's more productive and a lot more fun to respond creatively than to react cantankerously. Each moment, if we're awake to it, is an expansion of our knowledge and an encounter with our ignorance.

And I guess that I just don't know
And I guess that I just don't know.

—LOU REED

Nothing is written in stone, and even stones crumble in time. We make our best estimate of what's right and useful, and we do it. Any dope or fanatic can go full throttle if he's convinced he's doing the absolute will of God; it takes a mensch to act wholeheartedly when he knows he may turn out to have been completely misguided.

Your thoughts are just thoughts. They're not you—they're a sort of baggage you've picked up somewhere along the way—so you're not diminished when they turn out to be wrong. (Most people share their parents' politics. They rarely consider that, had they been born to the couple next door, they might hold opposite convictions with equal passion.) Why not dare to find out you were wrong, dare to "lose face"? Oops, there goes my face! What's left when your face is lost? Open space, freedom, what in Zen is called "the face you had before your parents met": your pristine, original nature, not obscured by an iron mask of rigid convictions. When you give up the need to "stand your ground"— to guard your little dirt pile of accidental opinions—you can go anywhere.

HAIL, HAIL, FREEDONIA!

The punch line of the joke is that life has no substantial reality. As we've seen, it's all connect-the-dots. It really happens, but there's no "it" to happen and no one for it to happen to. Everything is, as

171

one Zen practitioner described it, "like a reflection of the moon on a lake, with no moon and no lake, only reflection." This is the cosmic gag that all the saints and buddhas are in on. It's why, for example, the Dalai Lama can work so strenuously to save his crushed nation yet always seem to be floating through circumstances with superfluid humor and grace; he typifies the combination described by the Prajnaparamita Sutra as "skillful nonchalance and ceaseless concern."

Even the heaviest of burdens, when its dots have been disconnected, is infinitely light. The discrepancy between those two realities—the undeniable horrors that take place in the world of form and their indescribable lightness when all form is seen to be empty—leaves us with little to do but laugh. And then roll up our sleeves and, still chuckling, get back to work. Because form is emptiness, we enjoy the joke. Because emptiness is form, we act like mensches. It's all just a movie, but play your part flawlessly. It is (as one of my teachers put it) like having cold water running on one hand and hot water on the other. To be sane you've got to have both.

The movie that's most pertinent here is the Marx Brothers' *Duck Soup*. The make-believe nation of Freedonia, of which Groucho has somehow become leader, has its full panoply of ambassadors and generals who take themselves very seriously, but we know they're strictly for laughs. Villains conspire to take over the country, but we know there's nothing to take over: it's all imaginary, as blatantly insubstantial as Groucho's greasepaint mustache. Everything cancels itself out. (Embarking on a spy mission, Chico and Harpo are told, "If you're found, you're lost.") News of impending war normally inspires terror, but in Freedonia the more frantic the blowing of bugles and singing of anthems becomes, the more comically backward

it all seems ("To war we're going to go!"), and the more clearly is revealed how hilariously empty of reality it all is.

In our lives as in the movie, the plots and wars go on despite our
realization, but *we're* as free as Freedonia. It's not just that growing
enlightenment makes us laugh; laughter makes us grow more enlightened. It instantly shrinks the exaggerated seriousness of our
problems by making us relax our fixation on them. Perhaps that's
why comedy deals so insistently with the varieties of our pain, from
the primitive eye-poking of the Three Stooges to the existential angst
of Woody Allen. As Lama Surya Das says, "Enlighten up." Reach
outside the frame of your cartoon, grab a big mallet, and bust up
that crust of seriousness.

When my brothers and I made funny faces as little boys do, our
Grandma Sylvia would go into a deep, serious scowl and say, "If you
keep it up, your face will freeze like that!" And *her* face froze like *that!*
I just watched my cat Molly amuse herself for several minutes with
a single kernel of stray cat chow—stalking it, pouncing on it, bat-
ting it around the kitchen floor. Play with your food, play with your
life. You're the grown-up now; nobody's gonna ground you. Most
important, goof on yourself, loosen the surface tension that connects the dots of "I," play with your precious self-image. Whack it
around, air out some of the pomposity, hurl the cream pie into your
own face, if necessary be your own Larry, Moe, *and* Curly.

When we laugh, our attention is drawn down out of the head
and shoulders, where we usually carry tension, to the belly, where we
register contentment. Laughter boosts the production of endor-
phins (natural tranquilizers and pain blockers) and immune cells.
Twenty seconds of laughing provides a cardiovascular workout
equivalent to three minutes of strenuous exercise. Circulation and

oxygen consumption rise dramatically, and organs from the brain to the spleen receive a kind of internal massage. So our final practice technique is almost the most important: make sure you laugh every day, even when (*especially* when) you feel there's nothing to laugh about. One way to guarantee your daily laugh is to stand with your knees bent, slap them with both hands, then straighten up and throw your hands back as you shout, "Ho, ho, ho!" Keep going till the sheer stupidity of what you're doing makes you *really* laugh.

Both the West and the East have big-bellied embodiments of this attitude: Santa Claus and the laughing buddha Hotei. Each is pictured as wandering the land with a sack of goodies for children, signifying that laughter restores both our sense of generosity and our childlike innocence. I suspect that Jesus and Muhammad and Buddha didn't accumulate all those followers by being sourpusses; I think they were a lot of fun to be around. I think they busted their students' chops regularly and tried to grab people's hats, even if later editors of the scriptures expunged those stories as unbecoming the august dignity of the founders.

It has been said that "This world is a comedy to those that think, a tragedy to those that feel." That sounds backward to me. It's the thinking mind that sets up impossible expectations (that our enemies should be kind and rational, that those we love should live forever, that shit should not happen) and then is disappointed when its appointments go tragically unmet. The feeling heart, in concert with its neighbor the belly, certainly registers grief and fear but also taps into that far deeper level of experience, that ocean of silence from which roll waves of all-resolving, all-absolving, all-dissolving laughter.

DANCING NOWHERE

So, as jokester mensches, we act with utmost conscientiousness even while laughing at cosmic absurdity, on whatever epic or tiny stage we find ourselves—whether struggling, like the Dalai Lama and Bishop Tutu, to free an oppressed nation, or merely remembering to rinse our plate and put it in the dishwasher. Certainly there's a big quantitative difference in the impact of those acts, but qualitatively it's the same positive radiance, a.k.a. love. Anyway, a hundred or a thousand years from now the specific effects of our acts will be wiped out, but the momentum of positivity, the intensification of the current of the lovestream through the lives of all beings, has its subtle continuity.

Gandhi said that no matter what we do, it will be completely unimportant, but it is vitally important that we do it. Absolutely, nothing matters; relatively, everything matters. The trick is to live both of those truths deeply, all the time. Life may be a dance that goes nowhere. But it doesn't *need* to go anywhere—here it is. And if we can dance impeccably, without missing a step, yet with joyful abandon, it's a good dance.

PRACTICE

A final word before you're off to the next book . . .

How do you get to that luminous space of liberation, the kingdom of heaven which is always at hand? The same way you get to Carnegie Hall. Practice! Reading books is great, but if we don't find a way to integrate the practices into our lives we can wind up like those world Scrabble champions they've got in Thailand who've memorized the English dictionary but can't speak a lick of it.

I think any form of practice can get you there if you take it all the way. The reality is that you're going to do whatever you're going to do, which may or may not have anything to do with what you've read here. That's fine. But to learn from your choice, to make it at least a valid experiment, take it all the way. The great Tibetan meditation hero Milarepa said, "It is the tradition of the fortunate seekers never to be content with partial practice." Saint Paul said, "Whatsoever you do, do it heartily."

It doesn't matter that we're ordinary people and they were saints. They didn't start out that way. Milarepa was a murderer, and Paul was a persecutor of saints. They proved with their own lives that anyone can make it, and so deprived the rest of us of the excuse that our case is hopeless. Just find some method that has juice in it for you, and do it as if your life depended on it. Actually, much more than your life depends on it.

Once, when my daughter was two or three, we were at some kind of party or other—it was outdoors, in a big tent—and I tried to blow up a balloon for her. But it must have been the kind that you can't fill without a helium tank. Tara watched me huff and puff for awhile, then said, "Oh, Papa, do it like your *bones* would come out!"

Whatever you do, do it like your bones would come out.

APPENDIX:
ATTENTION! AT EASE!

*I have discovered that all human evil comes from
this, man's being unable to sit still in a room.*

—PASCAL

Peace of mind?

It's a piece of cake!

—DAVID BYRNE

How do you meditate?

Don't meditate. Just sit and give up.

Give up hope of doing it right and fear of doing it wrong. There's nothing to do. If you've learned some technique of meditation that you find effective, that's fine. But at some point the technique should transcend itself; meditating should dissolve into just being.

Why sitting?

Because when we lie down we tend to become less alert, and when we stand we tend to become less relaxed. What's left is sitting up comfortably, paying full attention yet completely at ease.

OK, so I sit. What else?

Nothing else.

Just sit. That's it.

Let the mind rest in its own natural state, which is exactly the state it's already in.

Let go of hashing out the past or planning for the future. Just rest in present awareness.

Rest in the skylike nature of mind, within which momentary thoughts and sense impressions come and go. No pushing, no pulling, no ignoring. Just relax and be aware.

Should I close my eyes?

Actually, your eyes are always open. It's your eye*lids* that open and close, and even when they're closed you see some color, light, and change, so it doesn't much matter. Most people, especially in the beginning, feel more settled with eyelids closed. Eventually, though, it's better to leave them open and relax into your natural widescreen gaze—like being at the movies, where you don't stare at any one part of the screen but effortlessly take it all in.

Don't worry about being distracted, since there's no point of focus to be distracted from. The cooking smells, the barking dog, whatever you're tempted to reject—*that's* the "object of meditation" (along with everything else), that's the kingdom of heaven on earth to which we are opening.

The stone that the builders rejected has become the keystone.

—PSALM 118

Our "task" is simply to rest in openness to the entire scope and variety of the kingdom, without rejecting or favoring anything. Let it all pass through you frictionlessly, as if you were transparent.

But I keep having thoughts.

Of course. It's as natural for the mind to think thoughts as it is for the ear to hear sounds. As thoughts arise (including any thoughts about how to "meditate"), let *them* pass through you as well.

Letting go of a thought is different from pushing it away. Simply relax your grip on it and open again to the totality of the present moment's experience. There's no need to clear the mind of thoughts, even if you could. In the face of thoughts, just continue to be.

If thoughts arise, remain present in that state.
If no thoughts arise, remain present in that state.
There is no difference in the presence in either state.

—GARAB DORJE

People often say they "can't meditate" because their mind is "a jumble of thoughts," but in the present moment there's no time for a jumble. We think just one thought at a time. Let *that* one go.

Still, though, the mind may sometimes be so agitated that you keep getting *lost* in thoughts, completely carried away by long trains of them. Then you can do the deep sigh described on page 13 again, or provide a little more structure by lightly favoring one of the senses:

179

- Gaze (not stare) into the palms of your hands, or at a spot on the ground, or at a rock, a flower, the surface of a pond, or any other object, passively resting your mind along with your gaze.
- Listen, paying easy attention to each multilayered moment of sound: traffic noise, wind in trees, air conditioner, near or distant voices.
- Note the tactile sense, the feeling of being in this body, in this seat.
- Use mantra (see page 105).
- Do guru yoga (page 72) or image gazing (page 102).
- Follow the movement of the breath.

In fact, especially at first, you may want to routinely begin each session with this more structured kind of practice; then, toward the end, let it melt into unstructured openness.

And what should happen?

What happens is we give up looking for something special to happen. No cosmic insights, no mystic visions: just regular, ordinary awareness. Every time you find yourself looking for something else, relax again, open to this moment's experience as it already is, like taking off a tight shoe. *Ahhh!*

Is there a special way to begin or end a session?

It's good to easily look around the room or the area where you're sitting, to sort of make friends with your environment and give the air a chance to settle. Then start with some kind of conscious breathing, such as the sighing technique. For a more deluxe ride, put your right thumb alongside your right nostril, close it, and slowly breathe out through your left nostril. Then in. Then close the left nostril with your third and fourth fingers, open the right nostril, and slowly breathe out through the right nostril. Then in. Continue in that pattern—out, in, switch, out, in, switch—for several minutes. Make each in-breath deep and complete, feeling your ribs separate and your torso expand in all directions, like a balloon being inflated; on the out-breath, deflate completely, contracting the abdominal muscles.

At the end of the session come out slowly, as the contrast can otherwise be a bit jarring. Stretch, ease back into activity. You can also take a moment to mentally share the benefit of your practice with all others.

How often should I sit?

If you want to taste freedom, sit from time to time. If you want to *live* freedom, sit every day. It's good to have a regular practice time so that it's part of your daily schedule. You can start with short sessions of about ten or fifteen minutes; later they'll tend to lengthen naturally. If you're having a leisurely weekend or a day at the beach (or a week in the hospital or a year in jail), you can sit more.

But once you're actually sitting, give up the idea of sitting in time, of practicing, say, for half an hour or even two minutes, like measuring out so many cups of beans. Only practice for one moment: *this* moment, then this moment, then this moment, till it's time to get up.

Is there a particular attitude I should assume?

Yes—drop your attitude. There's nothing to be formal or solemn about. Or take the attitude, "Here goes nothing." Relax: no one's grading you. It's hard if you make it hard, it's easy if you take it easy.

What's wrong with the word "meditation"?

Oh, too many syllables. It sounds like something complicated. Sometimes the M-word is unavoidable, but it's safer to keep it in quotation marks, to remind us that there's no such thing as meditation, there's only leaving all things as they are. Otherwise we tend to make meditation a *new* thing, by generating a subtle tension—a sort of crust—as if to tell ourselves, "OK, now I'm really meditating." That's a good time to make funny faces, shout "Ooga booga!," break up that crust.

The M-word also makes too much of an artificial distinction between formal sitting practice and every-moment-walking-around practice. It keeps us looking to master some sort of trick. But it's the one thing to which there's no trick. We just sit till we run out of tricks, till we tire of hopping around from one tricky strategy to another. (Silly rabbit—tricks are for kids!)

In this sense, teaching meditation is the world's simplest job. There's nothing to teach. You could just say one thing—

> *Whatever's there,*
> *Just rest aware.*

—and say it for the rest of your life, because people don't believe you. Immediately they start making exceptions: "Ah, he means whatever's there *except* the flies buzzing around the room, *except* the thoughts buzzing around my mind, *except* the lawnmower or the leaf-blower or the headache or boredom or bliss." Meditation, if it's anything, is the journey from "except"-ing to accepting. If there's silence, rest in silence; if there's noise, rest in noise; if you're tranquil, rest in tranquility; if you're restless, rest in restlessness.

But . . . I'm still confused.

Don't worry. Just sit and give up trying to understand. Once on a retreat, my teacher gave a very subtle explanation of sitting. A student raised her hand. "I'm confused—" she began, clearly about to launch into a long paragraph or two delineating the precise nature of her confusion. The teacher cut her off immediately and said, "Can you rest in *that*?"

SELECTED
BIBLIOGRAPHY

Abbot, Edwin A. *Flatland: A Romance of Many Dimensions*. Mineola, NY: Dover, 1992.

Chögyam, Ngakpa. *Spectrum of Ecstasy: Embracing Emotions as the Path of Inner Tantra*. NY & London: Aro, 1997.

Hixon, Lex. *Mother of the Buddhas: Meditation on the Prajnaparamita Sutra*. Wheaton, IL: Quest, 1993.

Meyer, Marvin. *The Gospel of Thomas: The Hidden Sayings of Jesus*. NY: HarperCollins, 1992.

Mitchell, Stephen, ed. *The Enlightened Heart: An Anthology of Sacred Poetry*. NY: HarperPerennial, 1993.

Mitchell, Stephen. *The Gospel According to Jesus: A New Translation and Guide to His Essential Teachings for Believers and Unbelievers*. NY: HarperPerennial, 1993.

Nyoshul Khenpo Rinpoche and Lama Surya Das. *Natural Great Perfection: Dzogchen Teachings and Vajra Songs*. Ithaca, NY: Snow Lion, 1995.

Plato. *The Symposium*. London: Penguin, 1951.

Sarno, John. *Healing Back Pain*. NY: Warner Books, 1991.

Sogyal Rinpoche. *The Tibetan Book of Living and Dying*. NY: HarperSanFrancisco, 1992.

CREDITS

ABOUT THE AUTHOR

Dean Sluyter has trained and practiced in several meditative and spiritual traditions and has taught nonsectarian approaches to meditation since 1970. An award-winning former film critic, he also teaches English at The Pingry School, where he has developed the innovative Literature of Enlightenment program for more than twenty years. He and his wife, artist Maggy Sluyter, live in New Jersey and have two grown children.